BENJAMIN FRANKLIN

The Way to Wealth

and Other Writings on Finance

BENJAMIN FRANKLIN

The Way to Wealth

and Other Writings on Finance

Edited with an Introduction by WALTER ISAACSON

Sterling Publishing Co., Inc.
New York

Library of Congress Cataloging-in-Publication Data Available

2 4 6 8 10 9 7 5 3

Published by Sterling Publishing Co., Inc.
387 Park Avenue South, New York, NY 10016
© 2006 by The Reference Works, Inc. and
Sterling Publishing Co., Inc.
Introduction © 2006 by Walter Isaacson and The Reference Works, Inc.
"Main Events in Franklin's Life" timeline © 2003 by SparkNotes LLC
Distributed in Canada by Sterling Publishing
c/o Canadian Manda Group, 165 Dufferin Street
Toronto, Ontario, Canada M6K 3H6
Distributed in the United Kingdom by GMC Distribution Services
Castle Place, 166 High Street, Lewes, East Sussex, England BN7 1XU
Distributed in Australia by Capricorn Link (Australia) Pty. Ltd.
P.O. Box 704, Windsor, NSW 2756, Australia

Produced by The Reference Works, Inc.
Managing Editor, Pamela Adler
Interior design by Emily Baker

Manufactured in the United States of America
All rights reserved

Sterling ISBN-13: 978-1-4027-3789-3
ISBN-10 1-4027-3789-0

For information about custom editions, special sales, premium and
corporate purchases, please contact Sterling Special Sales
Department at 800-805-5489 or specialsales@sterlingpub.com.

Table of Contents

Introduction by Walter Isaacson   vii

Part I: Industry   1
Chapter 1: Planning   2
Chapter 2: Working   5

Part II: Frugality   15
Chapter 3: Saving   16
Chapter 4: Investing   23

Part III: Prudence   29
Chapter 5: Owning   30
Chapter 6: Protecting   46

Part IV: Reason   51
Chapter 7: Borrowing   52
Chapter 8: Paying Taxes   56

Part V: Wisdom   69
Chapter 9: Retiring   70
Chapter 10: Bequeathing   80

Part VI: *Poor Richard's Way to Wealth*   101

Main Events in Franklin's Life   135
Sources   141

DOING WELL BY DOING GOOD

Introduction by Walter Isaacson

Benjamin Franklin's maxims in *The Way to Wealth*, along with his other writings on personal finance, reflect the many delightful layers of the most modern of all our Founders. He was the original writer of how-to-succeed books. And even though he was not always early to bed or early to rise, he loved giving self-help tips on how we could all become healthy, wealthy, and wise.

But there is an important theme that we must be sure not to miss. Franklin's goal was not simply personal wealth. It was also—as Poor Richard tells us—to "do well by doing good." In other words, it is possible to become successful by helping others and benefiting the common good. Helping others is part of a virtuous cycle: it makes you more valuable to your community, helps you to serve both your neighbors and your Lord, and also rebounds to your personal credit. To pour forth benefits for the common good was divine, he said. Franklin has always been the founding father who winks at us. George Washington's colleagues found it hard to imagine touching the austere general on the shoulder, and we would find it even more so today. Jefferson and Adams are just as intimidating. But Ben Franklin, that ambitious urban entrepreneur, seems made of flesh rather than of marble, addressable by nickname, and he turns to us from history's stage with eyes that twinkle from behind those newfangled spectacles. He speaks to us, through his letters and hoaxes and autobiography, not with orotund rhetoric but with a chattiness and clever irony that is very contemporary. We see his reflection in our own time.

Franklin has a particular resonance in twenty-first-century America. A successful publisher and consummate networker with an inventive curiosity, he would have felt right at home in the information revolution. He had unabashed ambition to be part of an upwardly-mobile meritocracy. We can easily imagine having a beer with him after work, showing him how to use a BlackBerry or Treo, and sharing the business plan for a new venture. He would laugh at the latest joke about a priest and a rabbi, or about a farmer's daughter. We would admire both his earnestness and his self-aware irony. And we would relate to the way he tried to balance, sometimes uneasily, a pursuit of reputation, wealth, earthly virtues and spiritual values.

His story is a classic one of rags to riches. He ran away from the Puritan town of Boston to the much more tolerant city of brotherly love, Philadelphia. He arrived tired and bedraggled and with but a few coins in his pocket. But he soon found work in a print shop, and eventually he built a printing business of his own. He helped create the content to fuel it, then he franchised his businesses all up and down the colonial coast, and finally he created a postal system to act as his distribution system. It was a way to wealth worthy of any twenty-first-century media baron.

Franklin was a natural shopkeeper: clever, charming, astute about human nature, and eager to succeed. He became, as he put it, "an expert at selling." His printing and publishing business succeeded largely due to his charm and diligence. Franklin became an apostle of being—and, just as important, appearing to be—industrious. Even after he became successful, he made a show of personally carting the rolls of paper he bought in a wheelbarrow down the street to his shop, rather than having a hired hand do it.

He was also the consummate networker. He liked to mix his civic life with his social one, and he merrily leveraged both to further his business life. This approach was evident when he formed a club of young workingmen, in the fall of 1727 shortly after his return to Philadelphia, that was commonly called "The Leather Apron Club" and officially dubbed "The Junto."

Franklin's little club was composed of enterprising tradesmen and artisans, rather than the social elite who had their own fancier gentlemen's clubs. At first the members went to a local tavern for their Friday evening meetings, but soon they were able to rent a house of their own. There they discussed issues of the day, debated philosophical topics, devised schemes for self-improvement, and formed a network for the furtherance of their own careers.

The enterprise was typical of Franklin, who seemed ever eager to organize clubs and associations for mutual benefit, and it was also typically American. As the nation developed a shopkeeping middle class, its people balanced their individualist streaks with a propensity to form clubs, lodges, associations, and fraternal orders. Franklin epitomized this Rotarian urge and has remained, after more than two centuries, a symbol of it.

In his club of aspiring shopkeepers and artisans, Franklin laid out a guide for the type of conversational contributions each member could usefully make. The questions he chose were a model of mixed practicality, good works, and tips for success:

"What new story have you lately heard agreeable for telling in conversation?… Hath any citizen in your knowledge failed in his business lately, and what have you heard of the cause?… Have you lately heard of any citizen's thriving well, and by what means?… Have you lately heard how any present rich man, here or elsewhere, got his estate?… Do you know of any fellow citizen who has lately done a worthy action deserving praise and imitation?… Is there any man whose friendship you want and which the Junto or any of them can procure for you?… In what manner can the Junto or any of them assist you in any of your honorable designs?"

Franklin's historical reputation has been largely shaped, for disciples and detractors alike, by his account in his autobiography of the famous project he launched to attain "moral perfection." This rather odd endeavor, which involved sequentially practicing a list of virtues, seems at once so earnest and mechanical that one cannot help either admiring him or ridiculing him. As the novelist D. H. Lawrence later sneered: "He made himself a list of virtues, which he trotted inside like a gray nag in a paddock."

So it's important to note the hints of irony and self-deprecation in his droll recollection, written when he was 79, of what he wryly dubbed "the bold and arduous project of arriving at moral perfection." First, he made a list of twelve virtues he thought desirable, and to each he appended a short, and often revealing, definition:

Temperance: Eat not to dullness; drink not to elevation.

Silence: Speak not but what may benefit others or yourself; avoid trifling conversation.

Order: Let all your things have their places; let each part of your business have its time.

Resolution: Resolve to perform what you ought; perform without fail what you resolve.

Frugality: Make no expense but to do good to others or yourself; i.e., waste nothing.

Industry: Lose no time; be always employed in something useful; cut off all unnecessary actions.

Sincerity: Use no hurtful deceit; think innocently and justly, and, if you speak, speak accordingly.

Justice: Wrong none by doing injuries, or omitting the benefits that are your duty.

Moderation: Avoid extremes; forbear resenting injuries so much as you think they deserve.

Cleanliness: Tolerate no uncleanliness in body, clothes, or habitation.

Tranquility: Be not disturbed at trifles, or at accidents common or unavoidable.

Chastity: Rarely use venery but for health or offspring, never to dullness, weakness, or the injury of your own or another's peace or reputation.

A Quaker friend "kindly" informed him that he had left something off: Franklin was often guilty of "pride," the friend said, citing many examples, and could be "overbearing and rather insolent." So Franklin added "humility" as the thirteenth virtue on his list. "Imitate Jesus and Socrates."

Mastering all of these thirteen virtues at once was "a task of more difficulty than I had imagined," Franklin recalled. His greatest difficulty was with the virtue of order. He was a sloppy man, and he eventually decided that he was so busy and had such a good memory that he didn't need to be too orderly. He likened himself to the hurried man who goes to have his ax polished but after a while loses patience and declares, "I think I like a speckled ax best."

Humility was also a problem. "I cannot boast of much success in acquiring the reality of this virtue, but I had a good deal with regard to the appearance of it," he wrote. "There is perhaps no one of our natural passions so hard to subdue as pride; disguise it, struggle with it, beat it down, stifle it, mortify it as much as one pleases, it is still alive and will every now and then peep out and show itself." This battle against pride would challenge him—and amuse him—for the rest of his life. "Even if I could conceive that I had completely overcome it, I would probably be proud of my humility."

Franklin's focus was on traits that could help him succeed in this world, instead of ones that would exalt his soul for the hereafter. However, we must look at what he did as well as what he said. Benevolence was the underlying theme in his life. The most acceptable service to God is doing good to man, he would often say. So he turned his personal finance virtues into a quest for civic improvement as well.

Poor Richard's Almanack, which Franklin began publishing at the end of 1732, combined these two goals of his doing-well-by-doing-good philosophy: the making of money and the promotion of virtue. It became, in the course of its twenty-five-year run, America's first great humor classic. The beleaguered Richard Saunders and his nagging wife Bridget helped to define what would become a dominant tradition in American folk humor: the naively wicked wit and homespun wisdom of characters who seem to be charmingly innocent but are sharply pointed about the pretensions of the elite and the follies of everyday life.

Almanacs were a sweet source of annual revenue for a printer, easily outselling even the Bible (because they had to be bought anew each year). In format and style, Franklin's was like many other almanacs. The name Poor Richard, a slight oxymoron pun, echoed that of *Poor Robin's Almanack*, which was published by Franklin's brother James. Benjamin Franklin, however, added his own distinctive flair by using his pseudonym to permit himself some ironic distance.

Years later, Franklin would recall that he regarded his almanac as a "vehicle for conveying instruction among the common folk" and therefore filled it with proverbs that "inculcated industry and frugality as the means of procuring wealth and thereby securing virtue." At the time, however, he also had another motive, about which he was quite forthright. The beauty of inventing a fictional author was that he could poke fun at himself by admitting, only half in jest, through the pen of Poor Richard, that money was his main motivation. "I might in this place attempt to gain thy favor by declaring that I write almanacs with no other view than that of the public good; but in this I should not be sincere," Poor Richard began his first preface. "The plain truth of the matter is, I am excessive poor, and my wife... has threatened more than once to burn all my books and Rattling-Traps (as she calls my instruments) if I do not make some profitable use of them for the good of my family."

Richard and Bridget Saunders did, in many ways, reflect Benjamin and Deborah Franklin. In the almanac for 1738, Franklin had the fictional Bridget Saunders take a turn at writing the preface for Poor Richard. This was shortly after Deborah Franklin had bought her husband a china breakfast bowl, and it came at the time when Franklin's newspaper pieces were poking fun at the pretensions of wives who acquire a taste for fancy tea services. Bridget Saunders announced to the reader that year that she read the preface her husband had composed, discovered he had "been slinging some of his old skits at me," and tossed it away. "Cannot I have a little fault or two but all the country must see it in print! They have already been told at one time that I am proud, another time that I am loud, and that I have a new petticoat, and abundance of such kind of stuff. And now, forsooth! all the world must know that Poor Dick's wife has lately taken a fancy to drink a little tea now and then." Lest the connection be missed, she noted that the tea was "a present from the printer."

Poor Richard's delightful annual prefaces never, alas, became as famous as the maxims and sayings that Franklin scattered in the margins of his almanacs each year, such as the most famous of all: "Early to bed and early to rise, makes a man healthy, wealthy and wise." Franklin would have been amused by how faithfully these were praised by subsequent advocates of self-improvement, and he would likely have been even more amused by the humorists who later poked fun at them. In a sketch with the ironic title "The Late Benjamin Franklin," Mark Twain jibed: "As if it were any object to a boy to be healthy and wealthy and wise on such terms. The sorrow that that maxim has cost me, through my parents, experimenting on me with it, tongue cannot tell. The legitimate result is my present state of general debility, indigence, and mental aberration. My parents used to have me up before nine o'clock in the morning sometimes when I was a boy. If they had let me take my natural rest where would I have been now? Keeping store, no doubt, and respected by all." Groucho Marx, in his memoirs, also picked up the theme. "'Early to bed, early to rise, makes a man you-know-what.' This is a lot of hoopla. Most wealthy people I know like to sleep late, and will fire the help if they are disturbed before three in the afternoon... You don't see Marilyn Monroe getting up at six in the morning. The truth is, I don't see Marilyn Monroe getting up at any hour, more's the pity."

Most of Poor Richard's sayings were not, in fact, totally original, as Franklin freely admitted. They "contained the wisdom of many ages and nations," he said in his autobiography, and he noted in the final edition of *Poor Richard* "that not a tenth part of the wisdom was my own." Even a near version of his "early to bed and early to rise" maxim had appeared in a collection of English proverbs a century earlier.

Franklin's talent was inventing a few new maxims and polishing up a lot of older ones to make them pithier. For example, the old English proverb "Fresh fish and new-come guests smell, but that they are three days old" Franklin made: "Fish and visitors stink in three days." Likewise, "A muffled cat is no good mouser" became "The cat in gloves catches no mice." He took the old saying "Many strokes fell great oaks" and gave it a sharper moral edge: "Little strokes fell great oaks." He also sharpened "Three may keep a secret if two of them are away" into "Three may keep a secret if two of them are dead." And the Scottish saying that "A listening damsel and a speaking castle shall never end with honor" was turned into "Neither a fortress nor a maidenhead will hold out long after they begin to parley."

In his final edition, completed while on his way to become an envoy for the colonies in England in 1757, Franklin summed things up with a speech by a fictitious character, an old man named Father Abraham who strings together all of Poor Richard's adages about the need for frugality and virtue. But Franklin's wry tone was, even then, still intact.

Poor Richard, who is standing in the back of the crowd, reports at the end: "The people heard it, and approved the doctrine, and immediately practiced the contrary."

All of this made Poor Richard a success and his creator wealthy. The almanac sold 10,000 copies a year. Father Abraham's speech compiling Poor Richard's sayings was published as *The Way to Wealth* and became, for a time, the most famous book to come out of colonial America. Within forty years, it was reprinted in 145 editions and seven languages; the French one was entitled *La Science du Bonhomme Richard*. Through the present, it has gone through more than 1,300 editions, plus now this new edition you hold in your hands.

Like Franklin's moral perfection project and *Autobiography*, the sayings of Poor Richard have been criticized for revealing the mind of a penny-saving prig. "It has taken me many years and countless smarts to get out of that barbed wire moral enclosure that Poor Richard rigged up," wrote D. H. Lawrence. But that misses the humor and irony, as well as the nice mix of cleverness and morality, that Franklin deftly brewed. It also mistakenly confuses Franklin with the characters he created. The real Franklin was not a moral prude, and he did not dedicate his life to accumulating wealth. "The general foible of mankind," he told a friend, is "in the pursuit of wealth to no end."

Rather than being a penny-pincher, Franklin used his success as a printer—and his wealth from Poor Richard's almanacs—to launch a variety of community organizations, including a lending library, fire brigade, and night watch-men corps, and later a hospital, militia, and college. "The good men may do separately," he wrote, "is small compared with what they may do collectively."

In *The Way to Wealth* and other such writings, Franklin indeed provides a good guide on how to become rich. But in his life and in his letters, he provides a good guide on how to be more than just rich. His mother, back in Boston, asked him why he was devoting so much of his time to his civic endeavors. His answer was a treatise on his personal theology. He believed strongly, he said, in the religious doctrine of salvation through good works, not merely through God's grace alone.

He ended that letter with a pithy credo that summed up his philosophy for his mother. "I would rather have it said," he wrote, "'He lived usefully,' than, 'He died rich.'" Because Poor Richard had taught him the art of doing well by doing good, it turned out that both things could be said about him when he died at the (unusual for his time) age of 84.

Walter Isaacson is the author of *Benjamin Franklin: An American Life*.

PART I

Industry

1

PLANNING

"You will never live long enough to learn everything that you need to know to succeed in life." This was a profound expression of Franklin's humility and practicality. It is crucial to learn from others while understanding that your own reasoning must help you understand what to do with what you learn from them. It is necessary to take your life into your own hands and take responsibility for your actions, because no one cares more about you than you do. You are the only one who can maintain control of your livelihood while aspiring to a life of wealth. It is thus critical to plan what you desire from life and how to get it, starting with a plan for your financial future. The importance of making a plan for your financial future is philosophical in nature, because until you start taking action, you will not know the outcome of your decisions. Benjamin Franklin spent a lot of time planning his actions as he traveled through life on his way to wealth. The following passages show examples of this journey.

Planning

He who lives on hope will die fasting.

Diligence is the mother of good luck.

Employ thy time well if thou meanest to gain pleasure.

Have you something to do tomorrow, do it today.

Lost time is never found again.

Many without labor would live by their wits only, but they break for want of stock.

Industry need not wish.

❧

CAPITALISM

"Is not the hope of one day being able to purchase and enjoy luxuries a great spur to labor and industry?"

❧

HOW TO GET RICHES

Benjamin Franklin wrote these maxims in 1749 as part of Poor Richard Improved *(the later incarnation of* Poor Richard's Almanack*). It appeared with a piece on sound.*

The art of getting riches consists very much in Thrift. All men are not equally qualified for getting money, but it is in the power of every one alike to practice this Virtue.

He that would be beforehand in the World, must be beforehand with his Business: It is not only ill Management, but discovers a slothful Disposition, to do that in the Afternoon, which should have been done in the Morning.

Useful Attainments in your Minority will procure Riches in Maturity, of which Writing and Accounts are not the meanest.

Learning, whether Speculative or Practical, is, in Popular or Mixt Governments, the Natural Source of Wealth and Honour.

> Precept I
> In Things of moment, on thy self depend,
> Nor trust too far thy Servant or thy Friend:
> With private Views, thy Friend may promise fair,
> And Servants very seldom prove sincere.

> Precept II
> What can be done, with Care perform to Day,
> Dangers unthought-of will attend Delay;
> Your distant Prospects all precarious are,
> And Fortune is as fickle as she's fair.

> Precept III
> Nor trivial Loss, nor trivial Gain despise;
> Molehills, if often heap'd, to Mountains rise:
> Weigh every small Expence, and nothing waste,
> Farthings long sav'd, amount to Pounds at last.

POVERTY

"Having been poor is no shame, but being ashamed of it is."

2

WORKING

It is important to realize that all a person has is the product of his or her labor. There are advantages and benefits of identifying oneself with what one does—and yet, not equating the person with that profession. Franklin was known as a writer and printer of Poor Richard's Almanack, *but he had many other activities and careers to make him the well-rounded individual that he was. Not only was his printing business important to him, but it was important for it to grow to support him and his family and to support his other pursuits. When he saw that his grandson Benjamin was developing a talent for the printing industry, he brought him on board to teach him its ways. Franklin discusses the details involved in working in his writings "Salaries in Arrears," "The True Story of Wealth and Plenty," and "Advice to a Young Tradesman, Written by an Old One."*

He that have a trade hath an estate.

Handle your tools without mittens; the cat in gloves catches no mice.

Sloth like rust consumes faster than labor wears; while the used key is almost bright.

He that have a calling hath an office of profit and honor.

Early to bed and early to rise makes a man healthy, wealthy and wise.

Laziness travels so slowly that Poverty soon overtakes him.

At the working man's house, hunger looks in but does not enter.

If we are industrious, we shall never starve.

❧

SALARIES IN ARREARS

In this letter to Joseph Galloway, Benjamin Franklin addresses his agency salaries that were to be delayed. The money from Massachusetts, £400, was not received until after the Revolution broke out, and the money from Georgia, £100 (later £200), was still unsettled as of November 1783. Franklin wrote this piece to question what was happening with his pending income.

London, January 6, 1773

Dear Friend:

I have received your favours of October 18 and 30. I am obliged greatly to you and Mr. Rhoads for your friendly interposition in the affair of my salary. As I never made any bargain with the House, I accept thankfully whatever they please to give me, and shall continue to serve them as long as I can afford to stay here. Perhaps it may be thought that my other agencies contribute more than sufficient for that purpose, but the Jersey allowance, though well paid, is a very small one; that from Georgia, £100 only, is some years in arrear; and will not be continued, as their appointment is by a yearly act, which I am told the governor will not again pass with my name in it. And from Boston I have never received a farthing, perhaps never shall, as their governor is instructed to pass no salary to an agent whose appointment he has not assented to. In these circumstances, with an almost double expense of living by my family remaining in Philadelphia, the losses I am continually suffering in my affairs there though absence, together with my now advanced age, I feel renewed inclinations to return and spend the remainder of my days in private life, having had rather more than my share of public bustle. I only wish first to improve a little, for the general advantage of our country, the favourable appearances arising from the change of our American minister, and the good light I am told I stand in with the successor. If I be instrumental in [illegible] things in good train, with a prospect of their [illegible] on a better footing than they have had for some years past, I shall think a little additional time well spent, though I were to have no allowance for it at all.

I must, however, beg you will not think of retiring from public business. You are yet a young man, and may still be greatly serviceable to your country. It would be, I think, something criminal to bury in private retirement so early all the usefulness of so much experience and such great abilities. The people do not indeed always see their friends in the same favourable light; they are sometimes mistaken, and sometimes misled; but sooner or later they come right again, and redouble their former affection. This, I am confident, will happen in your case, as it often has in the case of others. Therefore, preserve your spirits and persevere, at least to the age of sixty—a boundary I once fixed for myself, but have gone beyond it.

I am afraid the bill, Wilcock on Col. Alex. Johnstone, for £166 15 3 1/2 must be returned with a protest. I shall know in a day or two.

I shall consult Mr. Jackson, and do in the island affair what shall be thought best for securing your interest and that of all concerned.

By your spring ships I shall write you more fully. At present I can only add that I am with unalterable esteem and affection, yours most sincerely…

❧

THE TRUE SOURCES OF WEALTH AND PLENTY

Franklin spent time in London during the years 1757 to 1775. During this time he wrote to Timothy Folger, his cousin and a Nantucket whaling ship captain.

London, Sept. 29, 1769

Loving Kinsman,

Since my Return from abroad, where I spent part of the Summer, I have received your Favours of June 10 and July 26. The Treasury Board is still under Adjournment, the

Lords and Secretaries chiefly in the Country; but as soon as they meet again, you may depend on my making the Application you desire.

I shall enquire concerning the Affair of your two Townships settled under Massachusetts Grants, and let you know my Sentiments as soon as I can get proper Information. I should imagine that whatever may be determin'd here of the Massachusetts Rights to Jurisdiction, the private Property of Settlers must remain secure. In general I have no great Opinion of Applications to be made here in such Cases. It is so much the Practice to draw Matters into Length, put the Parties to immense Charge, and tire them out with Delays, that I would never come from America hither with any Affair I could possibly settle there.

Mrs. Stevenson sends her Love, and thanks you for remembering her. She is vex'd to hear that the Box of Spermaceti Candles is seiz'd; and says if ever she sees you again, she will put you in a way of making Reprisals. You know, she is a Smuggler upon Principle; and she does not consider how averse you are to every thing of the kind. I thank you for your kind Intention. Your Son grows fine Youth; he is so obliging as to be with us a little when he has Holidays; and Temple is not the only one of the Family that is fond of his Company.

It gives me great Pleasure to hear that our People are steady in their Resolutions of Non Importation, and in the Promoting of Industry among themselves. They will soon be sensible of the Benefit of such Conduct, tho' the Acts should never be repeal'd to their full Satisfaction. For their

Earth and their Sea, the true Sources of Wealth and Plenty, will go on producing; and if they receive the annual Increase, and do not waste it as heretofore in the Gewgaws of this Country, but employ their spare time in manufacturing Necessaries for themselves, they must soon be out of debt, they must soon be easy and comfortable in their circumstances, and even wealthy. I have been told, that in some of our County Courts heretofore, there were every quarter several hundred actions of debt, in which the people were sued by Shopkeepers for money due for British goods (as they are called, but in fact evils). What a loss of time this must occasion to the people, besides the expense, And how can Freeman bear the thought of subjecting themselves to the hazard of being deprived of their personal liberty at the caprice of every petty trader, for the paltry vanity of tricking out himself and family in the flimsy manufactures of Britain, when they might by their own industry and ingenuity, appear in good substantial honourable homespun! Could our folks but see what numbers of Merchants, and even Shopkeepers here, make great estates by American folly; how many shops of A, B, C and Co. with wares for exportation to the Colonies, maintain, each shop three or four partners and their families, every one with his country-house and equipage, where they live like Princes on the sweat of our brows; pretending indeed, sometimes, to wish well to our Privileges, but on the present important occasion few of them affording us any assistance: I am persuaded that indignation would supply our want of prudence, we should disdain the thralldom, we have so long been held in by this mischievous

10

commerce, reject it for ever, and seek our resources where God and Nature have placed them WITHIN OUR SELVES.

Your Merchants on the other hand, have shown a noble disinterestedness and love to their country, unexampled among Traders in any other age or nation, and which does them infinite honour all over Europe. The corrupted part indeed of this people here can scarce believe such virtue possible. But perseverance will convince them, that there is still in the world such a thing as public spirit. I hope that, if the oppressive Acts are not repealed this winter, your Stocks, that us'd to be employed in the British Trade, will be turned to the employment of Manufacturers among yourselves; For notwithstanding the former general opinion that manufacturers were impractible in America, on account of the dearness of labour, experience shows, in the success of the manufactures of paper and stockings in Pennsylvania, and of womens shoes at Lynn in your province, that labour is only dear from the want of CONSTANT employment by importations, the cheapness of our provisions gives us such advantage over the Manufactures in Britain, that (especially in bulky goods, whose freight would be considerable) we may always UNDERWORK THEM.

ADVICE TO A YOUNG TRADESMAN, WRITTEN BY AN OLD ONE

Franklin wrote this piece during his time in Philadelphia in 1748. It was printed at the New Printing Office. In it Franklin discusses how to be a good paymaster. He writes,

"In short, the way to wealth, if you desire it, is as plain as the way to market. It depends chiefly on two words, industry and frugality; that is waste neither time nor money, but make the best of both. Without industry and frugality, nothing will do, and with them everything."

To my friend A. B.

As you have desired it of me, I write the following Hints, which have been of Service to me, and may, if observed, be so to you.

Remember that TIME is Money. He that can earn Ten Shillings a Day by his Labour, and goes abroad, or sits idle one half of that Day, tho' he spends but Sixpence during his Diversion or Idleness, ought not to reckon That the only Expence; he has really spent or rather thrown away Five Shillings besides.

Remember that CREDIT is Money. If a Man lets his Money lie in my Hands after it is due, he gives me the Interest, so much as I can make of it during that Time. This amounts to a considerable Sum where a Man has good and large Credit and makes good Use of it.

Remember that Money is of a prolific generating Nature. Money can beget Money, and its Offspring can beget more, and so on. Five Shillings turn'd, is Six: Turn'd again, Seven and Three Pence; and so on 'til it becomes an Hundred Pound. The more there is of it, the more it produces every Turning, so that the Profits rise quicker and quicker. He that kills a breeding Sow, destroys all her Offspring to the thousandth Generation. He that murders a Crown, destroys all it might have produc'd, even Scores of Pounds.

Remember that Six Pounds a Year is but a Groat a Div. For this little Sum (which may be daily wasted either in Time or Expence unperceiv'd) a Man of Credit may on his own Security have the constant Possession and Use of an Hundred Pounds. So much in Stock briskly turn'd by an industrious Man, produces great Advantage.

Remember this Saying, That the good Paymaster is Lord Of another Man's Purse. He that is known to pay punctually and exactly to the Time he promises, may at any Time, and on any Occasion, raise all the Money his Friends can spare. This is sometimes of great Use: Therefore never keep borrow'd Money an Hour beyond the Time you promis'd, lest a Disappointment shut up your Friend's Purse forever.

The most trifling Actions that affect a Man's Credit, are to be regarded. The Sound of your Hammer at Five in the 'morning or Nine at Night, heard by a Creditor, makes him easy Six Months longer. But if he sees you at a Billiard Table, hears your Voice in a Tavern, when you should be at Work, he sends for his Money the next Day. Finer Cloathes than he or his Wife wears, or greater Expence in any particular than he affords himself, shocks his Pride, and he duns you to humble you. Creditors are a kind of People, that have the sharpest Eyes and Ears, as well as the best Memories of any in the World.

Good-natur'd Creditors (and such one would always choose to deal with if one could) feel Pain when they are oblig'd to ask for Money. Spare 'em that Pain, and they will love you. When you receive a Sum of Money, divide it among 'em in Proportion to your Debts. Don't be asham'd of paying a small Sum because you owe a greater. Money, more or less, is always welcome; and your Creditor had rather be at the Trouble of receiving Ten Pounds voluntarily brought him, tho' at ten different Times or Payments, than he oblig'd to go ten Times to demand it before he can receive it in a Lump. It shows, besides, that you are mindful of what you owe; it makes you appear a careful as well as an honest Man; and that still encreases your Credit.

Beware of thinking all your own that you possess, and of living accordingly. 'Tis a mistake that many People who have Credit fall into. To prevent this, keep an exact Account for Sonic Time of both your Expences and Your Incomes. If you take the Pains at first to mention Particulars, it will have this good Effect; you will discover how wonderfully small trifling Expences mount up to large Sums, and will discern what might have been, and may for the future be saved, without Occasioning any great Inconvenience.

In short, the Way to Wealth, if you desire it, is as plain as the Way to Market. It depends chiefly on two Words, INDUSTRY and FRUGALITY; i.e. Waste neither Time nor Money, but make the best Use of both. He that gets all he can honestly, and saves all he gets (necessary Expences excepted) will certainly become RICH; If that Being who governs the World, to whom all should look for a Blessing on their Honest Endeavours, doth not in his wise Providence otherwise determine.

PART II

Frugality

3

SAVING

Saving is the key to accumulating wealth. It is important to realize the orientation of wealth—saving, and to realize that saving money is not a luxury but a necessity of life as the central and most basic economic activity. There are many different ways to save. Many magazines today offer advice on the subject. However, it is important to keep in mind that embarking on these saving techniques needs to be done in the most logical, deliberate way.

Franklin was often journeying on his road to wealth with saving always playing an important role. As one driven to achieve success, Franklin did more than anyone else to lay the groundwork for building wealth and savings. He discusses his ideas for saving in "Money Entering Philadelphia" and "Prudential Algebra."

God helps those that help themselves.

Fly pleasures and they will follow you.

At a great pennyworth, pause awhile.

Saving

MONEY ENTERING PHILADELPHIA

In Part One of Franklin's Autobiography, *he writes about the importance of having money when entering Philadelphia. Though he had very little, he was generous with it.*

I have been the more particular this Description of my Journey. And shall be so of my first Entry into that City, that you may in your Mind compare such unlikely Beginning with the Figure I have since made there. I was in my working Dress, my best Clothes being to come round by Sea. I was dirty from my Journey; my Pockets were stuff'd out with Shirts and Stockings; I knew no Soul, nor where to look for lodging. I was fatigu'd with Travelling, Rowing and Want of rest. I was very hungry, and my whole Stock of Cash consisted of a Dutch Dollar and about a Shilling in Copper. The latter I gave the People of the Boat for my Passage, who at first refus'd it on Account of my Rowing; but I insisted on their taking it, a man being sometimes more generous when he has but a little Money than when he has plenty, perhaps thro' Fear of being thought to have but little. Then I walk'd up the Street, gazing about, till near the Market House I met a Boy with Bread. I had made many a Meal on Bread, and inquiring where he got it, I went immediately to the Baker's he directed me to in Second Street; and ask'd for Biscuit, intending such as we had in Boston, but they it seems were

17

not made in Philadelphia, then I ask'd for a three-penny Loaf, and was told they had none such: so not considering or knowing the Difference of Money and the greater Cheapness nor the Names of his Bread, I bad him give me three pennyworth of any sort. He gave me accordingly three great Puffy Rolls. I was surpris'd at the Quantity, but took it, and having no Room in my Pockets, walk'd off, with a Roll under each Arm, and eating the other. Thus I went up Market Street as far as Fourth Street, passing by the Door of Mr. Read, my future Wife's Father, when she standing at the Door saw me, and thought I made as I certainly did a most awkward ridiculous Appearance. Then I turn'd and went down Chestnut Street and part of Walnut Street, eating my Roll all the Way, and coming round found myself again at Market Street Wharf, near the Boat I came in, to which I went for a Draught of the River Water, and being fill'd with one of my Rolls, gave the other two to a Woman and her Child that came down the River in the Boat with us and were waiting to go farther. Thus refresh'd I walk'd again up the Street, which by this time had many clean dress'd People in it who were all walking the same Way; I join'd them, and thereby was led into the great Meeting House of the Quakers near the Market. I sat down among them, and after looking round a while and hearing nothing said, being very drowsy thro' Labour and want of Rest the preceding Night, I fell fast asleep, and continu'd so till the Meeting broke up, when one was kind enough to rouse me. This was therefore the first House I was in or slept in, in Philadelphia.

Walking again down towards the River, and looking in the Faces of People, I met a young Quaker Man whose Countenace I lik'd, and accosting him requested he would tell me where a Stranger could get Lodging. We were then near the Sign of the Three Mariners. Here, says he, is one Place that entertains Strangers, but it is not a reputable House; if thee wilt walk with me, I'll show thee a better. He brought me to the Crooked Billet in Water Street. Here I got a Dinner. And while I was eating it, several sly Questions were ask'd of me, as it seem'd to be suspected from my youth and Appearance, that I might be some Runaway. After Dinner my Sleepiness return'd: and being shown to a Bed, I lay down without undressing, and slept till Six in the Evening; was call'd to Supper; went to Bed again very early and slept soundly till the next Morning. Then I made myself as tidy as I could, and went to Andrew Bradford the Printer's. I found in the Shop the old Man his Father, whom I had seen in New York, and who traveling on horse-back had got to Philadelphia before me. He introduc'd me to his Son, who receiv'd me civilly, gave me a Breakfast, but told me he did not at present want a Hand, being lately supplied with one. But there was another Printer in town lately set up, one Keimer, who perhaps might employ me; if not, I should be welcome to lodge at his House, and he would give me a little Work to do now and then till fuller Business should offer.

The old Gentleman said, he would go with me to the new Printer: And when we found him, Neighbor, says Bradford, I have brought to see you a young Man of your Business, perhaps you may want such a One. He ask'd me a few Questions, put a Composting Stick in my Hand to see how I work'd, and then said he would employ me soon, tho' he had just then nothing for me to do. And taking old Bradford whom he had never seen before, to be one of the Townspeople that had a Goodwill for him, enter'd into a Conversation on his present Undertaking and Prospects; while Bradford not discovering that he was the other Printer's Father; on Keimer's Saying he expected soon to get the greatest Part of the Business into his own Hands, drew him on by artful Interest he relied on, and in what manner he intended to proceed. I who stood by and heard all, saw immediately that one of them was a crafty old Sophister, and the other a mere Novice. Bradford left me with Keimer, who was greatly surpris'd when I told him who the old Man was.

CASH

There are three faithful friends: an old wife, an old dog, and ready money.

SAVINGS

A penny saved is a penny earned.

A man may—if he knows not how to save as he gets—keep his nose to the grindstone.

When the well is dry, they know the worth of water.

For age and want, save while you may; no morning sun lasts a whole day.

❧

FRUGALITY

He that burns logs that cost nothing is twice warmed.

If you would be wealthy, think of Saving as well as of Getting.

Beware of little Expences; a small Leak will sink a great Ship.

A fat Kitchen makes a lean Will.

Fools make Feasts, and wise Men eat them.

What maintains one vice, would bring up two Children.

❧

PRUDENTIAL ALGEBRA

Joseph Priestley, who was invited to become librarian for the Earl of Shelburne, asked Franklin's advice on the theories of electricity. Both Franklin and Priestly were amateur scientists, but both contributed enormously to the field of science. Here is Franklin's reply, written from London on September 19, 1772. In it, Franklin, rather than offering advice, shares his method on how Priestley could advise himself using what he called "prudential algebra."

Dear Sir:

In the affair of so much importance to you wherein you ask my advice, I cannot, for want of sufficient premises, advise you

21

what to determine, but if you please I will tell you how. When these difficult cases occur, they are difficult chiefly because while we have them under consideration, all the reasons pro and con are not present to the mind at the same time; but sometimes one set present themselves, and at other times another, the first being out of sight. Hence the various purposes or inclinations that alternately prevail, and the uncertainty that perplexes us.

To get over this, my way is to divide half a sheet of paper by a line into two columns; writing over the one Pro, and over the other Con. Then during three or four days' consideration I put down under the different heads short hints of the different motives that at different times occur to me, for or against the measure. When I have thus got them all together in one view, I endeavour to estimate their respective weights; and where I find two (one on each side) that seem equal, I strike them both out. If I find a reason pro equal to some two reasons con, I strike out the three. If I judge some two reasons con equal to some three reasons pro, I strike out the five; and thus proceeding I find at length where the balance lies; and if after a day or two of further consideration, nothing new that is of importance occurs on either side, I come to a determination accordingly. And though the weight of reasons cannot be taken with the precision of algebraic quantities, yet when each is thus considered separately and comparatively, and the whole lies before me, I think I can judge better, and am less likely to make a rash step; and in fact I have found great advantage from this kind of equation, in what may be called moral or prudential algebra.

Wishing sincerely that you may determine for the best, I am ever, my dear friend, yours most affectionately.

4

INVESTING

*The cornerstone of building personal wealth is the invest-
ment of capital. Fundamentally, it takes money to make
more money, and to start this process, a small portion of
your savings should always be invested for future wealth.
There are many different kinds of investment tools. It is
important to look upon these precisely as tools or instruments, and to develop a knowledge in them in order to
determine which ones are best for you.*

'Tis easier to build two chimneys than to keep one in fuel.

Plow deep, while sluggards sleep, and you shall have
corn to sell and to keep.

Constant dripping wears away stone.

By diligence and patience the mouse ate in two the cable.

The diligent spinner has a large shift.

There are no gains without pains.

Money can beget money.

Frugality

⁂

GROWING INCOME

Franklin began writing Part Three of his autobiography at home in 1788. Many of his papers had been lost in the war, being pillaged by British troops. However, enough were preserved for him to be able to write his autobiography. Franklin earned about 750 pounds a year from his newspaper between 1748 and 1765, when approximately 25 percent of its circulation went to out-of-town subscribers. This provided him with enough income to allow him to invest in other endeavors. Here, in this piece from his autobiography, Franklin talks of such endeavors.

My Business was now continually augmenting, and my Circumstances growing daily easier, my Newspaper having become very profitable, as being for a time almost the only one in this and the neighboring Provinces. I experienc'd too the Truth of the Observation, that, *after getting the first hundred Pound, it is more easy to get the second*: Money itself being of a prolific Nature: The Partnership at Carolina having succeeded, I was encourag'd to engage in others, and to promote several of my Workmen who had behaved well, by establishing them with Printing Houses in different Colonies, on the same Terms with that in Carolina. Most of them did well, being enabled at the End of our Term, Six Years, to purchase the Types of me; and go on working for themselves, by which means several Families were raised.

Partnerships often finish in Quarrels, but I was happy in this, that mine were all carried on and ended amicably; owing I think a good deal to the Precaution of having very explicitly settled in our Articles everything to be done by or expected from each Partner, so that there was nothing to dispute, which Precaution I would therefore recommend to all who enter into Partnerships, for whatever Esteem Partners may have for and Confidence in each other at the time of the Contract, little Jealousies and Disgusts may arise, with Ideas of Inequality in the Care and Burden of the Business, etc. which are attended often with Breach of Friendship and of the Connection, perhaps with Lawsuits and other disagreeable Consequences.

MONEY TALKS

Franklin wrote this letter to Edward Bridgen, a British coin-maker and a friend of the American colonies, from Passy on October 2, 1779. In it, he suggests that the American coins feature a pious moral.

Dear Sir

I received your favour of the 17th past, and the 2 Samples of Copper are since come to hand. The Metal seems to be very good, and the Price reasonable, but I have not yet received the orders necessary to justify my making the purchase proposed. There has indeed been an Intention to strike Copper Coin that may not only be useful as small Change, but serve other purposes. Instead of repeating continually upon every Halfpenny the dull Story that everybody knows, and what it would have been no loss to mankind if no body had ever known, that George III is king of Great Britain, etc. to put one side some important proverbs of Salomon, some pious moral, prudential or Economical Precept, the frequent Inculcation of which by seeing it every time one receives a Piece of money might make an Impression upon the mind Especially of young persons and tend to regulate the Conduct; such as on some the fear of the Lord is the Beginning of wisdom; on others honesty is the best Policy; on others he that by the Plow would thrive; himself must either lead or drive, on others keep thy Shop and thy Shop will keep thee; on others A Penny sav'd is a Penny got, on others, he that buys what he has no need of will soon be forc'd to sell his necessaries, on others, Early to rise, will make a Man healthy wealthy and Wise and so on to a great variety. The other side it was propos'd to fill with good designs drawn and engrav'd by the Best artists in France of all the different Species of Barbarity with which the English have carry'd on the War in America expressing every abominable Circumstance of their Cruelty and inhumanity, that the figures can express, to make an Impression on the Minds of Posterity as Strong and durable as that on the Copper. This Resolution has been along time forborne, but the late Burning deffenceless Towns in Connecticut, on the flimsey Pretence that the People fired from behind their houses, when it is known

26

to have been premeditated and ordered from England, will probably give the finishing Provocation and may occasion a vast Demand for your Metal.

I thank you for your kind Wishes respecting my Health. I return them most cordially four fold into your own Bosome. Adieu.

B. Franklin

PART III

Prudence

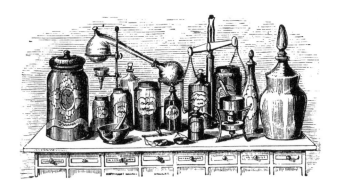

5

OWNING

It is valuable to have a proprietary stake with significant monetary value in one's work. The Franklinesque approach to ownership is seen to extend beyond "real" property to individual items of value in the modern world—information, intellectual property, and media—and is therefore even more relevant today than it was in the eighteenth century.

Franklin discusses the importance of owning things for their monetary value as well as their sentimental value in letters from his autobiography.

He that by the plow would thrive,
Himself must either hold or drive.

If you would have your business done, go; if not, send.

Keep thy shop, and thy shop will keep thee.

Pride that dines on vanity, soon sups on contempt.

Fond pride of dress is sure a very curse;
Ere fancy you consult, consult your purse.

The eye of a master will do more than both his hands.

Drive thy business, let not it drive thee.

Wealth is not his that has it, but his that enjoys it.

❦

FROM POOR RICHARD, MARCH 1736

*Franklin's autobiography, from which these letters are
excerpted, dealt with topics on the American Dream. He
wrote about the concept and its impact on wealth (amongst
other topics). Many condemned Franklin as materialistic
during his rise from rags to riches, but his musings are as
important as his actions on gaining wealth.*

*Poor Richard was stereotyped as being excessively con-
cerned with money, but the writings actually reveal Franklin's
own complex mind. Franklin never lost sight of his audience,
the farmer, or his purpose, selling almanacs.*

❦

TO WILLIAM STRAHAN, PHILADELPHIA, JUNE 2, 1750

*Franklin wrote to his friend William Strahan, a successful
London printer, of his disgust with "the Pursuit of Wealth to
no End."*

The Description you give of the Company and Manner of
Living in Scotland, would almost tempt one to remove
thither. Your Sentiments of the general Foible of Mankind,
in the Pursuit of Wealth to no End, are express'd in a
Manner that gave me great Pleasure in reading: They are

extremely just, at least they are perfectly agreeable to mine. But London Citizens, they say, are ambitious of what they call dying worth a great Sum: The very Notion seems to me absurd; and just the same as if a Man should run in debt for 1000 Superfluities, to the End that when he should be stript of all, and inprison'd by his Creditors, it might be said, he broke worth a great Sum. I imagine that what we have above what we can use, is not properly ours, tho' we possess it; and that the rich Man who must die, was no more worth what he leaves, than the Debtor who must pay.

❧

To Jane Mecom, London, December 30, 1770

While Franklin worked as joint Postmaster General of North America, he was accused of being "too much an American." He frequently outraged the Ministry because, although he held a patronage position, he did not work for the Ministry's supposed interests. On the other hand, some jealous American patriots occasionally impugned his motives and his actions because he enjoyed official patronage. His sister, Jane Mecom, expressed alarm about the latest rumor that he had been removed as Postmaster General. Here he explains his position to her.

As to the Rumour you mention (which was, as Josiah tells me, that I had been depriv'd of my Place in the Post Office on Account of a letter I wrote to Philadelphia) it might have this Foundation, that some of the Ministry had been displeas'd at my Writing such Letters, and there were really some Thoughts among them of strewing that Displeasure in that manner. But I had some Friends too, who unrequested by me advis'd the contrary. And my Enemies were forc'd to content themselves with abusing me plentifully in the Newspapers, and endeavouring to provoke me to resign. In this they are not likely to succeed, I being deficient in that Christian Virtue of Resignation. If they would have my Office, they must take it.

I have heard of some great Man, whose Rule it was with regard to Offices, *Never to ask for them*, and *never to refuse them*: To which I have always added in my own Practice, *Never to resign them*. As I told my Friends, I rose to that office thro' a long Course of Service in the inferior Degrees of it: Before my time, thro' bad Management, it never produced the Salary annex'd to it; and when I receiv'd it, no Salary was to be allow'd if the office did not produce it. During the first four Years it was so far from defraying itself, that it became £950 Sterling in debt to me and my Collegue. I had been chiefly instrumental in bringing it to its present flourishing State, and therefore thought I had some kind of Right to it. I had hitherto executed the Duties of it faithfully, and to the perfect Satisfaction of my Superiors, which I thought was all that should be expected of me on that Account.

As to the Letters complain'd of, it was true I did write them, and they were written in Compliance with another Duty, that to my Country. A Duty quite Distinct from that of Postmaster. My Conduct in this respect was exactly similar with that I held on a similar Occasion but a few Years ago, when the then Ministry were ready to hug me for the Assistance I afforded them in repealing a former Revenue Act. My Sentiments were still the same, that no such Acts should be made here for America; or, if made should as soon as possible be repealed; and I thought it should not be expected of me, to change my Political Opinions every time his Majesty thought fit to change his Ministers. This was my Language on the Occasion; and I have lately heard, that tho I was thought much to blame, it being understood that even Man who holds an Office should act with the Ministry whether agreable or not to his own judgment, yet in consideration of the goodness of my private Character (as they are pleas'd to compliment me) the office was not to be taken from rue. Possibly they may still change their Minds, and remove me; but no Apprehension of that sort, will, I trust, make the least Alteration in my Political Conduct.

My rule in which I have always found Satisfaction, is, Never to turn asside in Publick Affairs thro' Views of private Interest; but to go strait forward in doing what appears to me right at the time, leaving the Consequences with Providence. What in my younger Days enabled me more easily to walk upright, was, that I had a Trade; and that I could live upon a little; and thence (never having had views of making a Fortune) I was free from Avarice, and contented with the plentiful Supplies my business afforded me. And now it is still 'fore easy for me to preserve my Freedom and Integrity, when I consider, that I am almost at the End of my Journey, and therefore need less to complete the Expence of it; and that what I now possess thro' the Blessing of God may with tolerable Economy, be sufficient for me (great Misfortunes excepted) tho' I should add nothing more to it by any Office or Employment whatsoever.

❧

To Thomas Cushing, London, June 10, 1771

In direct violation of their instructions from England, some Royal and Proprietary officials passed popular measures in order to win high salaries from colonial assemblies, while other officials were kept in virtual poverty. The Crown react-ed by arranging payment for Royal officials directly from England. The Boston patriots saw this action as a threat to local self-rule. Franklin, as the Massachusetts Agent, tried in vain to prevent the change. In reporting his failure he philosophized about the nature of avarice.

I do not at present see the least likelihood of preventing the Grant of Salaries or Pensions from hence to the King's Officers in America, by any Application in Behalf of the People there, It is look'd on as a strange thing here to object to the King's paying his own Servants sent among us to do his Business; and they say we should seem to have much more Reason of Complaint if it were requir'd of us to pay them. And the more we urge the Impropriety of their not depend-ing on us for their Support, the More Suspicion it breeds that we are desirous of influencing them to betray the Interests of their Master or of his Nation. Indeed if the Money is rais'd from us against our Wills, the Injustice becomes more evident than where it arises from hence. I do not think, however, that the Effect of these Salaries is likely to be so considerable, either in favour of Government here, or in our Prejudice, as may generally apprehend. The love of Money is not a Thing of certain Measure, so as that it may be easily filled and satisfied, Avarice is infinite, and where there is not good economy, no Salary, however large, will prevent Necessity. He that has a fixed, and what others may think a competent Income, is often as much to be byassed by the Expectation of more, as jibe had already none at all. If the Colonies should resolve on giving handsome Presents to good Governors at or after their Departure, or to their Children after their Decease, I imagine it might produce even better Effects than our present annual Grants. But the Course probably will soon be, that the Chief Governor to whom the Salary is given, will have Leave to reside in England, a Lieutenant or Deputy will be left to do the Business and live on the Perquisites, which not being thought quite sufficient, his receiving Presents yearly will be wink'd at thro' the Interest of his Principal, and thus things will get into the old Train, only this Inconvenience remaining, that while by our Folly in consuming the Duty Articles, the fixed Salary is raised on ourselves without our Consent, we must pay double for the same Service. However, tho' it may be a hopeless Task while the Duties continue sufficient to pay the Salaries, I shall on all proper Occasions make Representations against this new Mode; and if by the Duties falling short, the Treasury here should be call'd on to pay those Salaries, it is possible they may come to be seen in another Light than at present, and dropt as unnecessary.

36

❧

To David Hartley, Passy, France, February 2, 1780

Franklin repeatedly risked his personal fortune in support of what he deemed justice for America. When the Boston Port Bill was before Parliament in 1774, Franklin himself engaged to pay the 15,000 pounds for the tea destroyed by the Boston Tea Party in order to prevent the passage of the bill. However, his proposal was rejected.

I am as much for peace as ever I was, and as heartily desirous of seeing the War ended, as I was to prevent its Beginning; of which your Ministers know I gave a strong Proof before I left England, when, in order to an accommodation, I offer'd at my own Risque, without Orders for so doing, and without knowing whether I should be own'd in doing it, to pay the whole Damage of destroying the Tea at Boston, provided the Acts made against that Province were repealed. This offer was refused. I still think it would have been wise to have accepted it.

❧

Benjamin Vaughan To Lord Shelburne, Dover, November 24, 1782

Benjamin Vaughan, Lord Shelburne's private secretary, acted as Shelburne's personal emissary in the Paris peace negotiations— no doubt because he was Franklin's friend and disciple. His letters to Shelburne record in detail his talks with the American peace commissioners, even when the discussions did not bear directly upon the peace negotiations. He thus reported Franklin's conversation concerning political equality among the rich, as well as Franklin's shrewd appraisal of the underlying economic reasons for past historical actions and his surprisingly modern view of the causes of poverty and oppression.

My lord,

I think it necessary to inform your lordship in a few words, that Dr. Franklin's opinions about parliaments are, that people should not be rejected as electors because they are at present ignorant or because their ignorance arises from their being excluded. He thinks that a statesman should meliorate his people; and I suppose would put this, among other reasons for extending the privilege of Election, that it would meliorate them. When the act to lessen the number of voters, passed in Edward the 3d's time, it was followed by an act to reduce wages; and he thinks that probably one act was made with a view to the other. On the other hand when knowledge began to spread in England, it helped everything, for instance, the post office revenue increased beyond all conception, while the same revenue in Ireland continues still as contemptible, as to be worth only a few thousand pounds. He says, that with themselves in America, they find no inconvenience in every man's voting that is free; and that the qualifications of a representative are matters sufficiently well distinguished by them. He says that savages would do the same, taking their best men as they can find them, and others forming themselves in business under them.

Perhaps your lordship will think all this too theoretical. When I return, I hope to have the honor of communicating his own expressions. As an American, the Dr. would choose to give no opinion of a different cast; but I believe, by some more positions he added to it, that this is his own genuine opinion. He thinks that the lower people are as we see them, because oppressed; and then their situation in point of manners, becomes the reason for oppressing them. But he is full of the measure of raising the sentiments and habits of all, as a thing that is wanting to contribute to the real sensible happiness of both orders the rich and the poor.

❦

To Robert Morris, Passy, France, December 25, 1783

Franklin's basic attitude toward wealth could be character-ized as radical. In eighteenth-century fashion, he related wealth to the origin of society and the basic rights of man. He reasoned that all wealth, in addition to that necessary for the basic requirements of subsistence, clothing, and shelter, was created by arbitrary conventions of society, and thus such wealth was at the disposal of society.

All Property, indeed, except the Savage's temporary Cabin, his Bow, his Matchboat, and other little Acquisitions, absolutely necessary for his Subsistence, seems to me to be the Creature of public Convention. Hence the Public has the Right of Regulating Descents, and all other Conveyances of Property, and even of limiting the Quantity and the Users of it. All the Property that is necessary to a Man, for the Conservation of the Individual and the Propagation of the Species, is his natural Right, which none can justly deprive him of: But all Property superfluous to such purposes is the Property of the Publick, who, by their Laws, have created it, and who may therefore by other Laws dispose of it, whenever the Welfare of the Publick shall demand such Disposition. He that does not like civil Society on these Terms, let him retire and live among Savages. He can have no right to the benefits of Society, who will not pay his Club towards the Support of it.

❧

To Benjamin Webb, Passy, France, April 22, 1784

Nowhere is Franklin's personal generosity better seen than in this letter to his acquaintance Benjamin Webb, a Kentucky senator and historian.

Dear Sir,

I received yours of the 15th Instant, and the Memorial it inclosed. The account they give of your situation grieves me. I send you herewith a Bill for Ten Louis d'ors. I do not pretend to give such a Sum; I only lend it to you. When you shall return to your Country with a good Character, you cannot fail of getting into some Business, that will in time enable you to pay all our Debts. In that Case, when you meet with another honest Man in similar Distress, you must pay me by lending this Sum to him; enjoining him to discharge the Debt by a like operation, when he shall be able, and shall meet with such another opportunity, I hope it may thus go thro' many hands, before it meets with a Knave that will stop its Progress. This is a trick of mine for doing a deal of good with a little money. I am not rich enough to afford much in good works, and so am obliged to be cunning and make the most of a little. With best wishes for the success of your Memorial, and your future prosperity. I am, dear Sir, your most obedient servant.

B. Franklin

❧

TO BENJAMIN VAUGHAN, PASSY, FRANCE, JULY 26, 1784

Luxury was a standard intellectual topic throughout the eighteenth century. Franklin's own complex attitudes toward luxury are set forth in his letter to Benjamin Vaughan. Here is its conclusion.

One reflection more, and I will end this long, rambling Letter. Almost all the Parts of our Bodies require some Expence. The Feet demand Shoes; the Legs, Stockings; the rest of the Body, Clothing; and the Belly, a good deal of Victuals. Our Eyes, tho' exceedingly useful, ask, when reasonable, only the cheap Assistance of Spectacles, which could not much impair our Finances. But the Eyes of other People are the Eyes that ruin us. If all but myself were blind, I should want neither fine Clothes, fine Houses, nor fine Furniture.

❧

PRIVATE PROPERTY IS A CREATURE OF SOCIETY, NOVEMBER, 1789

Franklin's final thoughts on the nature of wealth responded to a newspaper proposal in November 1789 on Pennsylvania's new state constitution. The anonymous author urged a bicameral legislature: "The Upper should represent the Property; the Lower the Population of the State. The Upper should be chosen by Freemen possessing in Lands and Houses one thousand Pounds; the Lower by all such as had resided four Years in the Country, and paid Taxes. The first should be chosen for four, the last for two years. They should in Authority be co-equal." In rebuttal, Franklin returned to the idea that wealth is created by the laws and customs of a society. Franklin probably intended to publish his reply and so he concluded with a supposed Biblical passage, which, although it echoes Jeremiah, is apparently his own creation.

Several Questions may arise upon this Proposition. 1st. What is the Proportion of Freemen possessing Lands and Houses of one thousand Pounds value, compared to that of Freemen whose Possessions are inferior? Are they as one to ten? Are they even as one to twenty? I should doubt whether they are as one to fifty. If this minority is to choose a Body expressly to controul that which is to be chosen by the great Majority of the Freemen, what have this great Majority done to forfeit so great a Portion of their Right in Elections? Why is this Power of Controul, contrary to the spirit of all Democracies, to be vested in a Minority, instead of a Majority? Then is it intended, or is it not, that the Rich should have a Vote in the Choice of Members for the lower House, while those of inferior Property are deprived of the Right of voting for Members of the upper House? And why should the upper House, chosen by a Minority, have equal Power with the lower chosen by a Majority? Is it supposed that Wisdom is the necessary concomitant of Riches, and that one Man worth a thousand Pounds must have as much Wisdom as Twenty who have each only 999; and why is Property to be represented at all? Suppose one of our Indian Nations should now agree to form a civil Society; each Individual would bring into the Stock of the Society little more Property than his Gun and his Blanket, for at present he has no other. We know, that, when one of them has attempted to keep a few Swine, he has not been able to maintain a Property in them, his neighbours thinking they have a Right to kill and eat them whenever they want Provision, it being one of their Maxims that hunting is free for all; the accumulation therefore of Property in such a Society, and its Security to Individuals in every Society, must be an Effect of the Protection afforded to it by the joint Strength of the Society, in the Execution of its Laws. Private Property therefore is a Creature of Society, and is subject to the Calls of that Society, whenever its Necessities shall require it, even to its last Farthing; its Contributions therefore to the public Exigencies are not to be considered as conferring a Benefit on the Publick, entitling the Contributors to the Distinctions of Honour and Power, but as the Return of an Obligation previously received, or the Payment of a just Debt. The Combinations of Civil Society are not like those of a Set of Merchants, who club their Property in different Proportions for Building and Freighting a Ship, and may therefore have some Right to vote in the Disposition of the Voyage in a greater or less Degree according to their respective Contributions; but the important ends of Civil Society, and the personal Securities of Life and Liberty, these remain the same in every Member of the society; and the poorest continues to have an equal Claim to them with the most opulent, whatever Difference Time, Chance, or Industry may occasion in their Circumstances. On these Considerations, I am sorry to see the Signs this Paper I have been considering affords, of a Disposition among some of our People to commence an Aristocracy, by giving the Rich a predominancy in Government, a Choice peculiar to themselves in one half the Legislature to be proudly called the UPPER House, and the other Branch, chosen by the Majority of the People, degraded by the Denomination of the LOWER; and giving to this upper House a Permanency of four Years, and but two to the lower. I hope, therefore, that our Representatives in the Convention will not hastily go into these Innovations, but take the Advice of the Prophet, "Stand in the old ways, view the ancient Paths, consider them well, and be not among those that are given to Change."

GENEROSITY

A man is sometimes more generous when he has but a little money than he who has plenty, perhaps through fear of being thought to have but little.

6

PROTECTING

It is prudent to know the essence of insurance as a way to protect your assets. It is crucial to have a rational plan for protecting what you own and what you will acquire. The means by which you provide protection grow naturally out of the basic philosophy of property and ownership. They are both presented and developed along similarly rational and prudent lines of thinking. Franklin advises us on protecting in "Beware of Being Lulled into a Dangerous Security."

For want of a nail the shoe was lost; for want of a shoe the horse was lost; and for want of a horse the rider was lost (being overtaken and slain by the enemy), all for want of care about a horseshoe nail.

> Great estates may venture more,
> But little boats should keep near shore.

> A little neglect may breed a great mischief.

> In the affairs of this world, men are saved not by faith, but by the want of it.

Want of care does us more damage than want of knowledge.

Three moves is as bad as a fire.

I never saw an oft-removed tree,
Nor yet an oft-removed family,
That thrived so well as those that settled be.

❧

THE HAT TRICK

Franklin once called on a rich Quaker friend who lived all by himself in an enormous house. As Franklin walked through the rooms of the mansion, he said, "Sir, why do you go to the cost of keeping up this immense house when you just need a fraction of the space?"

The rich man replied, "I have the means,"

Upon entering the dining room, Franklin saw a table that could seat twenty-five people. He asked, "Why such a large table?"

The wealthy man again answered, "I have the means."

"In that case," said Franklin, taking the hat from the Quaker's head, "why don't you have a hat big enough for twenty-five people? You have the means!"

❧

BEWARE OF BEING LULLED INTO
A DANGEROUS SECURITY

Franklin wrote to Charles Thomson, a political leader in the American Revolution, from Passy on May 13, 1784.

Thomson emigrated to America from Ireland in 1739. He was instrumental in obtaining the decision for the Great Seal of the United States.

Dear Sir,

Yesterday evening Mr. Hartley met with Mr. Jay and myself when the ratifications of the Definitive Treaty were exchanged. I sent a copy of the English Ratification to the President.

Thus the great and hazardous enterprise we have been engaged in is, God be praised, happily compleated; an event I hardly expected I should live to see. A few years of Peace, will improve, will restore and encrease our strentth; but our future safety will depend on our union and our virtue. Britain will be long watching for advantages, to recover what she has lost. If we do not convince the world, that we are a Nation to be depended on for fidelity in Treaties; if we appear negligent in paying our Debts, and ungrateful to those who have served and befriended us; our reputation, and all the strength it is capable of procuring, will be lost, and fresh attacks upon us will be encouraged and promoted by better prospects of success. Let us therefore beware of being lulled into a dangerous security; and of being both enervated and impoverished by luxury; of being weakened by internal contentions and divisions; of being shamefully extravagant in contracting private debts, while we are backward in discharging honorably those of the public; of neglect in military exercises and discipline, and in providing stores of arms and munitions of war, to be ready on occasion; for all these are circumstances that give confidence to enemies, and diffidence to friends and the expenses required to prevent a war are much lighter than those that will, if not prevented, be absolutely necessary to maintain it.

I am long kept in suspense without being able to learnt purpose of Congress respecting my request of recall, and that of some employment for my secretary, William Temple Franklin. If I am kept here another winter, and as much weakened by it as by the last, I may as well resolve to spend the remainder of my days here; for I shall be hardly able to bear the fatigues of the voyage in returning. During my long absence from America, my friends are continually diminishing by death, and my inducements to return in proportion. But I can make no preparations either for going conveniently, or staying comfortably here, nor take any steps towards making some provision for my grandson, till I know what I am to expect. Be so good, my dear friend, as to send me a little private information. With great esteem, I am ever yours, most affectionately.

PRUDENCE

'Tis easier to suppress the first Desire, than to satisfy all that follow it.

Pride that dines on Vanity sups on Contempt.

Pride breakfasted with Plenty, dined with Poverty, and supped with Infamy.

'Tis hard for an empty Bag to stand upright.

Get what you can, and what you get hold; 'tis the Stone that will turn all your Lead into Gold.

PART **IV**

Reason

7

BOROWING

Franklin discussed the destructive effects of borrowing and the ways of warding off the enticements of modern society that encourage borrowing in its many forms. There are many circumstances that justify borrowing and just as many options that a prudent individual should consider appropriate before embarking on borrowing of any kind. We live in a society that thinks nothing of borrowing, with debt and bankruptcy at an all-time high. It is necessary to understand your borrowing habits in order to find your way to wealth. Franklin teaches how in "Profit from Poor Richard" and "In Real and Great Want of Money."

Think what you do when you run in debt: you give another Power over your Liberty.

Rather go to bed supperless than rise in debt.

The borrower is a slave to the lender, and the debtor to the creditor.

Creditors are a superstitious sect, great observers of set days and times.

Creditors have better memories than debtors.

Lying rides upon debt's back.

If you would know the value of money, go try to borrow some, for he that goes a-borrowing, goes a-sorrowing.

If you will not hear reason, she'll surely rap your knuckles.

PROFIT FROM POOR RICHARD

The title Poor Richard's Almanack *originated from the name of a London almanac maker from the seventeenth century, Richard Saunders, and* Poor Robin, *a best-selling almanac from 1661 to 1776. Franklin's almanac,* Poor Richard, *sold a little over 10,000 copies a year, which at 4 pence each, provided Franklin a profit of about 5,000 pounds, a small fortune in late eighteenth-century America.*

In 1732 I first published my Almanac, under the Name of Richard Saunders; it was continu'd by me about twenty-five Years, commonly call'd *Poor Richard's Almanack.* I endeavor'd to make it both entertaining and useful, and it accordingly came to be in such Demand that I reap'd considerable Profit from it, vending annually near ten Thousand. And observing that it was generally read, scarce any Neighborhood in the Province being without it, I consider'd it as a proper Vehicle for conveying Instruction among the common People, who bought scarce any other Books. I therefore filled all the little Spaces that occur'd between Remarkable Days in the Calendar, with Proverbial

Sentences, chiefly such as inculcated Industry and Frugality, as the means of procuring Wealth and thereby securing Virtue, it being more difficult for a Man in Want to act always honestly, as (to use here one of those Proverbs) it is hard for an empty Sack to stand upright. These Proverbs, which contained the wisdom of many Ages and Nations, I assembled and form'd into a connected Discourse prefix'd to the Almanac of 1757, as the Harangue of a wise old Man to the People attending an Auction. The bringing all these scatter'd Counsels thus into a Focus enabled them to make greater Impression. The piece being universally approved was copied in all Newspapers of the Continent, reprinted in Britain on a Broadside to be stuck up in the Houses, two Translations were made of it in French, and great Numbers bought by the Clergy and Gentry to distribute gratis among their poor Parishioners and Tenants. In Pennsylvania, as it discouraged useless Expense in foreign Superfluities, some thought it had its share of Influence in producing that growing Plenty of Money which was observable for several Years after its Publication.

EXPENSES

"When people's incomes are lessened, if they cannot proportionately lessen their outgoings, they must come to poverty."

Borrowing

❧

In Real And Great Want Of Money

The partnership of Franklin and Francis Childs in New York had not gone well, and Childs had long put off paying Franklin what he owed for a bond. Franklin wrote a pressing letter to him from Philadelphia on April 27, 1789.

Sir:

You wrote me in December last that as soon as you returned from attending the Assembly you would immediately set out for Philadelphia in order to make a final settlement of our accounts. This was a promise very agreeable to me, as my late heavy expense in building five houses (which cost much more that I was made to expect) has so exhausted my finances that I am now in real and great want of money. I therefore send by my son Bache your bond which you were to discharge in January last. And I hope and entreat that as I have shown myself willing and ready to serve you, you will now in return exert yourself to serve me by paying off the debt, at a time when I so much want it; which will exceedingly oblige Your friend and humble servant...

Mr. Bache on payment will deliver up the bond and give you on my behalf any discharge you may think proper, which shall be as good as if given by me.

B.F.

8

PAYING TAXES

Franklin's approach to taxation is characteristically American. It is critical to consider taxes within the context of a personal financial strategy and to accept them and their need and place in American society. As much as taxes pose a challenge to gaining wealth, it is not prudent to enter into schemes to avoid paying them. Franklin discusses his desires for taxes and paper-currency in his "Essay on Paper-Currency, Proposing a New Method for Fixing Its Value" and "A Paper Currency Scheme."

We are taxed twice as much by our idleness, three times as much by our Pride, and four times as much by our folly.

Idleness taxes many of us much more, if we reckon all that is spent in absolute sloth.

Away then with your expensive follies, and you will not have so much cause to complain of hard times, heavy taxes, and chargeable families.

Gain may be temporary and uncertain, but even while you live, Expense is constant and certain.

❧

TIME IS MONEY

Franklin's printing shop in Philadelphia sold books. One day a man walked in and picked up a book. "How much is it?" he asked Franklin.

"Two shillings," was the reply.

The would-be purchaser demurred and haggled with Franklin over the cost. He then said to Franklin, "I'll give you only one shilling and sixpence."

Franklin replied, "The price is three shillings."

"What?" said the buyer. "You said earlier it was two shillings."

"The price is now three," said Franklin. "You have cost me in argument another shilling's worth of my time."

❧

ESSAY ON PAPER CURRENCY, PROPOSING A NEW METHOD FOR FIXING ITS VALUE

Franklin wrote of his plan for fixing the value of currency, then new to America. It helped him win a contract to print the Pennsylvania land bank notes, and laid the groundwork for the paper currency in use today.

It appears by the Resolutions of the Honourable the House of Commons of Great Britain, that it is their Opinion, that the Issuing Paper Currencies in the

American Colonies hath been prejudicial to the Trade of Great Britain, by causing a Confusion in Dealings, and lessening of Credit in those Parts; and that there is Reason to apprehend, that some Measures will be fallen upon, to hinder or restrain any future Emissions of such Currencies, when those that are now extant shall be called in and sunk. But if any Scheme could be formed, for fixing and ascertaining the Value of Paper Bills of Credit, in all future Emissions, it may be presumed such Restraints will be taken off, as the Confusion complained of in Dealings would thereby be avoided. Something of this Kind is here attempted, in hopes that it may be improved into a useful Project. But I shall first set down a few plain Remarks touching the Fluctuation of Exchange, and the Value of Gold and Silver in the Colonies; with some Observations on the Ballance of Trade; in order to render what follows the more clear and intelligible.

I. Even particular Man, that is concerned in Trade, whose Imports and Exports are not exactly equal, must either draw Bills of Exchange on other Countries, or buy Bills to send abroad to ballance his Accounts.

II. The Exports and Imports in any Colony, may be managed by different Hands, and the Number of those chiefly implored in the latter mar greatly exceed the Number of those implored in the former.

Hence it is evident there may sometimes be many Buyers and few Sellers of Bills of Exchange, even whilst the Exports may exceed in Value the Imports: And it is easy to conceive that in this Case, Exchange may rise.

III. The British Merchants, who trade to the Colonies, are often unacquainted with the Advantages that may be made building of Ships there, or by the Commodities of those Colonies carried to the West Indies, or to Foreign Markets: And for that Reason, frequently order all their Remittances in Bills of Exchange, tho' less advantageous; which must encrease the Demand for Bills, and enhance the Price of them.

IV. A great Demand in Europe for any of the Commodities of the Colonies, and large Orders for those Commodities from the British Merchants to their Factors here, with Directions to draw for the Value, may occasion Exchange to fall for a Time, even tho' the Imports should be greater than the Exports.

V. Hence it appears, that a sudden great Demand for Bills in the Colonies, may, at any time, advance the Exchange; and a sudden great Demand abroad for their Commodities may fall the Exchange.

VI. Gold and Silver will always rise and fall, very near in Proportion as Exchange rises and falls; being only wanted, in those Colonies that have a Paper Currency, for the same Use as Bills of Exchange, *viz.* for Remittances to England.

VII. When few People can draw on England, or furnish those who want Remittances with Gold or Silver, Paper Currency may fall with respect to Sterling-Money and Gold and Silver, (by which the British Merchants always judge it) and yet keep up to its original Value in Respect to all other Things.

VIII. From all these Considerations, I think, it appears that the Rising or Falling of the Exchange can be no sure Rule for Discovering on which Side the Balance of Trade lies; because that Exchange may be affected by various Accidents independent thereof. But in order to determine this Point with more Certainty, it should be considered;

IX. That whatever is imported, must, first or last, be paid for in the Produce or Manufactures of the Country: If the Commodities exported in one Year be not sufficient to pay for what is imported, the Deficiency must be made up by exporting more in succeeding Years; otherwise the Colony becomes Debtor for so much as the Deficiency is; which at last must be discharged (if it is ever discharged) by their Lands.

X. If this has been the Case with any Colony; or if the Debt of the Colony to Great Britain has been increasing for several Years successively, it is a Demonstration that the Ballance of Trade is against them: But on the Contrary, if the Debt to Great Britain is lessening yearly, or not increasing, it is as evident, that the Ballance of Trade is not against them; notwithstanding the Currency of that Colony may be falling gradually all the while.

I shall now, proceed to the Scheme for fixing the Value of a Paper Currency, *viz.*

XI. Let it be supposed, that in some one of the Colonies the Sum of 110,000 in Bills of Credit was proposed to be struck, and all other Currencies to be called in and destroyed; and that 133*l.* 6*s.* 8*d.* in these Bills should be equivalent to 100*l.* Sterling; which likewise would make the said Bills equal to Foreign Coins, at the Rates settled by the Act of Parliament made in the Sixth Year of Queen ANNE.

At which Rate, according to this Scheme, it may be as well settled as at any other.

XII. Let One Hundred Thousand Pounds be emitted on Loan, upon good Securities, either in Land or Plate, according to the Method used in Pennsylvania, the Borrowers to pay Five per Cent per Annum Interest, together with a Twentieth Part of the Principal, which would give the Government an Opportunity of sinking it by Degrees, if any Alteration in the Circumstances of the Province should make it necessary: But if no such Necessary appeared, so much of the Principal as should be paid in, might be re-emitted on the same Terms as before.

XIII. The other Ten Thousand Pounds to be laid out in such Commodities as should be most likely to yield a Profit at Foreign Markets, to be ship'd off on Account of the Colony, in order to raise a Fund or Bank in England: Which Sum, so laid out, would in two Years time, be returned into the Office again by the Interest Money.

XIV. The Trustees or Managers of this Bank to be impowered and directed to supply all Persons that should apply to them, with Bills of Exchange, to be drawn on the Colony's Banker in London, at the aforesaid Rate of 133*l.* 6*s.* 8*d.* of the said Bills of Credit for 100*l.* Sterling. The Monies thus brought in, to be laid out again as before, and replaced in England in the said Bank with all convenient Speed: And as these provincial Bills would have, at least, as good a Credit as those of any private Person; every Man, who had occasion to draw, would, of Course, be obliged to dispose of his Bills at the same Rate.

XV. It is by Means of this Bank, that it is proposed to regulate the Rate of Exchange; and therefore it would be necessary to make it so large, or procure the Trustees such a Credit London, as should discourage and prevent any mischievous Combinations for draining it and rendering the Design useless I know of no Inconvenience that could arise by allotting double the proposed Sum for that Service, but that the annual Interest would be lessen'd; which in some Governments has been found a useful Engine for defraying the publick Expence. But if only a Credit should be thought needful, over and above the said Sum, and upon some Emergency Recourse should be had to it, the Interest Money would soon afford sufficient Means for answering that Credit.

XVI. The Trustees might further be impowered and directed, to take in Foreign Coins, at the Rates prescribed by the Act of Parliament, from those who wanted to change them for Paper Currency, and to exchange for those who wanted Gold and Silver. This, it is imagined, might reduce those Coins again to a Currency, which now are only bought and sold as a Commodity. Or, if it should be judged more advantageous to the Credit of the Paper Currency, Part of the Proceeds of what should be sent abroad, might be returned to the Province in Gold and Silver, for creating a Fund here.

XVII. I hope it will appear upon examining into the Circumstances of the Paper Money Colonies, by the Rule proposed above, that the Ballance of Trade has not been so much against them as is commonly imagined; but that the Fall of their Currencies, with Respect to Sterling, and to

Gold and Silver, has been chiefly occasioned either by some such Accidents as are above shewed to influence it; which by this Scheme will be all prevented: Or to their being issued without any good Foundation for supporting their Credit, such as a Land Security, and company. However that be, I think, there can be no room, upon our Plan, to fear, that the Credit of the Paper Currency can be injur'd, even though the Ballance of Trade were against the Colony, while their Bank in London can be duely supported.

From the sad Consequence of a losing Trade, *viz.* that of having the Property of the Lands transferr'd to another Country, it appears absolutely necessary for every Colony, that finds or suspects that to be its own Case, to think timely of all proper Means for preventing it; such as encouraging Iron Works, Ship building, raising and manufacturing of Hemp and Flax, and all other Manufactures not prohibited by their Mother Country. They might likewise save considerable Sums, which are now sent to England, by setting up and establishing an Insurance Office. This, I think, might effectually he done by an Act of Assembly for impowering the Trustees of the Loan Office to subscribe all Policies that should he brought to them, on such Terms as should be settled by the said Trustees jointly with a Committee of Assembly, at a Meeting for that Purpose, once a Month, or oftener if necessary. Besides the saving to the Country in the Article of Trade, it would probably yield a considerable yearly Income towards the Support of Government; it being evident, that most prudent Insurers are great Gainers upon the Whole of their Insurances, after all Losses are deducted.

Upon the Execution of this Scheme, I am persuaded, two very great Advantages must accrue; First That the Export would he increased, and consequently bring the Ballance of Trade more in favour of the Province: And, Secondly, that the Rate of Exchange would be fixed and ascertained; which 'tis hoped, would effectually remove the Prejudices which the Merchants in England seem to have conceived against a Paper Currency in the Colonies.

~

A PAPER CURRENCY SCHEME

While the Stamp Act was under discussion, Franklin proposed a scheme for an American paper currency, as a kind of alternative to the pending tax laws. Nothing came of this plan, which the Americans would probably have liked no better than the Stamp Act. Franklin proposed the idea in a letter to Joseph Galloway, an American Loyalist leader, from London on October 11, 1766. Galloway entered the Pennsylvania assembly in 1756 and soon joined Franklin in petitioning the King to abolish the proprietary government of the Penns.

Dear Sir,

I received your Favour of Aug. 23, almost the only one I had by that Packet. It gives me great Pleasure to learn that our Friends keep up their Spirits, and that you have little doubt of the new Election. I have occasionally had several Conferences lately with our present Secretary of State, Lord Shelbourne, and some on the Affair of the Petitions. He was pleas'd to assure me that he was of Opinion Mr. Penn ought to part with the Government voluntarily, and said he had often told him so; but however that might be, he said that the Relation between them could and should have no Influence with him, in the Disputes subsisting between the Proprietors and People, as possibly some might suppose, and company—Mr Jackson is not yet come to Town, nor is the Season of Business yet come on; but nothing in my Power shall be wanting to push the Matter vigorously to a Conclusion if possible this Winter; for, besides my Concern for the Publick, I really want to be at home and at Rest.

You see by the late Papers that we have had several Changes in the Ministry this Summer. I was in hopes now Mr Pitt was in, that we should have had a Ministry more firm and durable; for really these frequent Changes are extreamly discouraging to all who have Business to transact with the Government:—but they begin now to whisper that we are not yet fix'd, and that before the Meeting of Parliament, we shall see fresh Overturnings. This, however, I do not give much Credit to. There may be some Changes, but I hope not considerable ones.

You take notice, that in the London Merchants Letter there is mention made of a Plan for a general Currency in America, being under Consideration of the Ministry; and you wish it may suit the Temper of the Americans. I will let you into the History of that Plan. When we were opposing the Stamp Act, before it pass'd, Mr. Grenville often threw out to us, that the Colonies had had Notice of it, and knew it would be necessary for Government here to draw some Revenue from them, and they had propos'd nothing that might answer the End and be more agreeable to themselves: And then he would say, Can you Gentlemen that are Agents name any Mode of raising Money for Publick Service that the people would have less Objection to, if we should agree to drop this Bill? This encourag'd me to present him with a Plan for a General Loan Office in America, nearly like ours, but with some Improvements effectually to prevent Depreciation; to be established by Act of Parliament, appropriating the Interest to the American Service, and company. This I then thought would be a lighter and more bearable Tax than the Stamps, because those that pay it have an Equivalent in the Use of the Money; and that it would at the same time furnish us with a Currency which we much wanted, and could not obtain under the Restrictions lately laid on us. Mr Greenville paid little Attention to it, being besotted with his Stamp Scheme, which he rather chose to carry through. But the Successors of that Ministry, when it fell into their Hands, took fancy to it, and a good deal of Pains in considering it, had frequent Conferences with me upon it, and really strengthened one another and their Friends in the Resolution of Repealing the Stamp Act, on a Supposition that by this Plan of a Loan Office they could raise a greater Sum with more satisfaction to the People.—However, when the Stamp Act was repeal'd, I did not press the other, but advis'd that when they had settled the Plan to their own Minds, they should send Copies to the several Governors and Assemblies in America, to the End they might receive all their Opinions, Objections and Improvements, that it might, whenever carried into Execution, be as perfect as possible, and, (it might be) with general Consent as it was a Matter of great Importance. In the meantime, I drew a Bill for our present Relief (at the Request of a Member) to take off the Restraint on our legal Tenders by the late Act. I send you a copy of it inclos'd. Nothing was done on it, the Session being nearly at an End. I wish for your Sentiments on it.

With this Bill among my Papers I find inclos'd Draft of a Petition I gave Mr Jackson to present against the Bill for extending to Scotland the Act for transporting Felons to America. He did not think fit to present it, (and indeed it was not fit to be presented without some Alterations which I purpos'd to make if it had been presented, it being rather too ludicrous) but he show'd it among the Members, and it occasion'd some Laughing; but it was said, the Way to get the Transportation of Felons abolish'd, would be for all the Colonies to remonstrate against it.

It is certainly high time, as you observe, that our publick Debts were discharged;—but I hope no Consideration of your Agents will induce the House to any Compliances inconsistent with the Publick Good, in order to obtain an Act for discharging those Debts.

As soon as any thing of consequence occurs, I shall not fail writing to the Committee. Present my Respects to them, and believe me ever, Dear Friend.

Affectionately yours,
B. Franklin

PART V
Wisdom

9

RETIRING

One needs to plan for one's later years; this is even more true today than in Franklin's time. People are living much longer today than ever before and need the financial means to afford to live as well later on. Any worthy financial plan needs to have at its core both the development of wealth and the preservation of wealth into the future. It is crucial to consider the ways in which to devise a retirement plan and how retiring should be viewed simply as a passage into another active phase of life. Franklin discusses his retirement plan in "Happiness in This Life," "Remembering a Song" and "Among the Felicities of My Life."

A Child and a fool imagine twenty years and twenty shillings can never be spent.

Work while it is called Today, for you know not how much you will be hindered Tomorrow.

Leisure is time for doing something useful; this leisure the diligent man will obtain, but the lazy man never.

A plowman on his legs is higher than a gentleman on his knees.

❧

Happiness in This Life

Franklin wrote this letter to Hugh Roberts, an old friend residing in Bucks County, Pennsylvania, from London on September 16, 1758, discussing what made him happy in life. Roberts was appointed title treasurer in examining Franklin's mortgage on the Daniel Boone farm.

Dear Friend,

Your kind Letter of June 1, gave me great Pleasure. I thank you for the Concern you express about my Health, which at present seems tolerably confirm'd by my late Journeys into different Parts of the Kingdom, that have highly entertaining as well as useful to me. Your Visits to my little Family in my Absence are very obliging, and I hope you will be so good as to continue them. Your Remark on the Thistle and the Scotch Motto, made us very merry, as well as your String of Puns. You will allow me to claim a little Merit or Demerit in the last, as having had some hand in making you a Punster; but the Wit of the first is keen, and all your own.

Two of the former Members of the Junto you tell me are departed this Life, Potts and Parsons. Odd Characters, both of them. Parsons, a wise Man, that often acted foolishly. Potts, a Wit, that seldom acted wisely. If Enough were the Means to make a Man happy, One had always the Means of Happiness without ever enjoying the Thing; the other had always the Thing without ever possessing the Means. Parsons, even in his Prosperity, always fretting! Ports, in the midst of his Poverty, ever laughing! It seems, then, that Happiness in this Life rather depends on Internals than Externals; and that, besides the natural Effects of Wisdom and Virtue, Vice and Folly, there is such a Thing as being of a happy or an unhappy Constitution. They were both our Friends, and lov'd us. So, Peace to their Shades. They had their Virtues as well as their Foibles; they were both honest Men, and that alone as the World goes, is one of the greatest of Characters. They were old Acquaintances, in whose Company I formerly enjoy'd a great deal of Pleasure, and I cannot think of losing them, without Concern and Regret.

Let me know in your next, to what Purposes Parsons will'd his Estate from his Family; you hint at something which you have not explain'd.

I shall, as you suppose, look on every Opportunity you give me of doing you Service, as a Favour, because it will afford me Pleasure. Therefore send your Orders for buying Books as soon as you please. I know how to make you ample Returns for such Favours, by giving you the Pleasure of Building me a House. You may do it without losing any of your own Time; it will only take some Part of that you now spend in other Folks Buisness. 'Tis only jumping out of their Waters into mine.

I am grieved for our Friend Syng's Loss. You and I, who esteem him, and have valuable Sons ourselves, can sympathise with him sincerely. I hope yours is perfectly recovered, for your sake as well as for his own. I wish he may be in every Respect as good and as useful a Man as his Father. I need not wish him more; and can now only add that I am, with great Esteem, Dear Friend, Yours affectionately.

P.S. I rejoice to hear of the Prosperity of the Hospital, and send the wafers.

I do not quite like your absenting yourself from that good old Club the Junto: Your more frequent PRESENCE might be a means of keeping them from being ALL ENgag'd in Measures not the best for the Publick Welfare. I exhort you therefore to return to your Duty and, as the Indians say, to confirm my Words, I send you a Birmingham Tile.

I thought the neatness of the Figures would please you.

Pray send me a good Impression of the Hospital Seal in Wax. 2 or three would not be a miss, I may make a good Use of them.

❧

REMEMBERING A SONG

The date of Franklin's letter to the Abbé Lefebvre de La Roche, a member of Madame Helvétius's circle at Auteuil and an old acquaintance, is not known. It was, however, originally print-ed in French. W. T. Franklin, Franklin's illegitimate son, pub-lished it with a translation in English. The song is a drinking song which Ben Franklin wrote on happiness.

I HAVE run over, my dear friend, the little book of poetry by M. Helvétius with which you presented me. The poem on Happiness pleased me much, and brought to my recollection a little drinking song which I wrote forty years ago upon the same subject, and which is nearly on the same plan with many of the same thoughts, but very concisely expressed. It is as follows:

Singer.
Fair Venus calls; her voice obey,
In beauty's arms spend night and day.
The joys of love all joys excel,
And loving's certainly doing well.

Chorus.
Oh! no!
Not so!
For honest souls know,
Friends and a bottle still bear the bell.

Singer.
Then let us get money, like bees lay up honey;
We'll build us new hives, and store each cell.
The sight of our treasure shall yield us great pleasure;
We'll count it, and chink it, and jingle it well.

Chorus.
Oh! no!
Not so!
For honest souls know,
Friends and a bottle still bear the bell.

Retiring

Singer.

If this does not fit ye, let's govern the city,
In power is pleasure no tongue can tell;
By crowds though you're teased, your pride shall be pleased,
And this can make Lucifer happy in hell!

Chorus.
Oh! no!
Not so!
For honest souls know,
Friends and a bottle still bear the bell.

Singer.

Then toss off your glasses, and scorn the dull asses,
Who, missing the kernel, still gnaw the shell;
What's love, rule, or riches? Wise Solomon teaches,
They're vanity, vanity, vanity still.

Chorus.
Oh! no!
Not so!
For honest souls know,
Friends and a bottle still bear the bell.

'Tis a singer, my dear Abbé, who exhorts his companions to seek happiness in love, in riches, and in power. They reply, singing together, that happiness is not to be found in any of these things; that it is only to be found in friends and wine. To this proposition the singer at last assents. The phrase "bear the bell," answers to the French expression, "obtain the prize."

I have often remarked, in reading the works of M. Helvétius, that, although we were born and educated in two countries so remote from each other, we have often been inspired with the same thoughts; and it is a reflection very flattering to me, that we have not only loved the same studies, but, as far as we have mutually known them, the same friends, and the same woman. Adieu! my dear friend, etc…

∽

AMONG THE FELICITIES OF MY LIFE

Franklin ended his last letter to Catherine Ray Greene, one of Franklin's closest female friends, almost exactly thirty-four years after his first letter to her, as if he knew this was his farewell. It was written from Philadelphia on March 2, 1789, and became part of his autobiography.

Dear Friend:

Having now done with public affairs, which have hitherto taken up so much of my time, I shall endeavour to enjoy, during the small remainder of life that is left to me, some of the pleasures of conversing with my old friends by writing, since their distance prevents my hope of seeing them again.

I received one of the bags of sweet corn you were so good as to send me a long time since, but the other never came to hand. Even the letter mentioning it, though dated

December 10, 1787, has been above a year on its way; for I received it but about two weeks since from Baltimore in Maryland. The corn I did receive was excellent, and gave me great pleasure. Accept my hearty thanks.

I am, as you suppose in the above mentioned old letter, much pleased to hear that my young friend Ray is "smart in the farming way," and makes such substantial fences. I think agriculture the most honourable of all employments, being the most independent. The farmer has no need of popular favour, nor the favour of the great; the success of his crops depending only on the blessing of God upon his honest industry. I congratulate your good spouse, that he, as well as myself, is now free from public cares, and that he can bend his whole attention to his farming, which will afford him both profit and pleasure; a business which nobody knows better how to manage with advantage.

I am too old to follow printing again myself, but, loving the business, I have brought up my grandson Benjamin to it, and have built and furnished a printing house for him, which he now manages under my eye. I have great pleasure in the rest of my grandchildren, who are now in number eight, and all promising, the youngest only six months old, but shows signs of great good nature. My friends here are numerous, and I enjoy as much of their conversation as I can reasonably wish; and I have as much health and cheerfulness as can well be expected at my age, now eighty three. Hitherto this long life has been tolerably happy; so that, if I were allowed to live it over again, I should make no objection, only wishing for leave to do what authors do in a second edition of their works, correct some of my errata. Among the felicities of my life I reckon your friendship, which I shall remember with pleasure as long as that life lasts, being ever, my dear friend, yours most affectionately…

To Cadwallader Colden, Philadelphia, September 29, 1748

Franklin was considered the most daring, innovative, skilled, and successful printer in America. He gave it all up in 1748. He explains his reasons for retirement in this letter to his friend, Cadwallader Colden, a philosopher, scientist, and Loyalist governor of New York.

Sir

I received your Favour of the 12th Inst. which gave me the greater Pleasure, as 'twas so long since I had heard from you. I congratulate you on your Return to your beloved Retirement: I too am taking the proper Measures for obtaining Leisure to enjoy Life and my Friends more than heretofore, having put my Printing house under the Care of my Partner David Hall, absolutely left off Bookselling, and remov'd to a more quiet Part of the Town, where I am settling my old Accounts and hope soon to be quite a Master of my own Time, and no longer (as the Song has it) at every one's Call but my own. If Health continues, I hope to be able in another Year to visit the most distant Friend I have, without Inconvenience. With the same Views I have refus'd engaging further in publick Affairs; The Share I had in the late Association, and company having given me a little present Run of Popularity, there was a pretty general Intention of choosing me a Representative for the City at the next Election of Assemblymen; but I have desired all my Friends who spoke to me about it, to discourage it, declaring that I should not serve if chosen. Thus you see I am in a fair Way of having no other Tasks than such as I shall like to give my self, and of enjoying what I look upon as a great Happiness, Leisure to read, study, make Experiments, and converse at large with such ingenious and worthy Men as are pleas'd to honour me with their Friendship or Acquaintance, on such Points as may produce something for the common Benefit of Mankind, uninterrupted by the little Cares and Fatigues of Business. Among other Pleasures I promise my self, that of Corresponding more frequently and fully with Dr. Colden is none of the least; I shall only wish that what must be so agreeable to me, may not prove troublesome to you.

10

BEQUEATHING

Connectedness with the future is an important human trait, no less so than one's connection to one's past. The financial aspects of bequeathing are seen as outgrowths of a lifetime of financial planning and strategy. Franklin made certain to account for everyone in his life, so that when he died they would enjoy the benefit of his wealth. He didn't just consider the immediate future world without him, he also considered what would happen many years later. He made it clear in "Service is No Inheritance" that one's duties to one's relatives will determine one's wealth, and not just one's relations. It cannot be assumed that one will inherit wealth; we must therefore strive to create it ourselves. Franklin's "Last Will and Testament" makes clear exactly what happened to his possessions and money—all part of his wealth.

Let not the sun look down and say, Inglorious here he lies.

Many estates are spent in the getting,
Since women for tea forsook spinning and knitting,
And men for punch forsook hewing and splitting.

Bequeathing

Learning is to the studious;
Riches to the careful;
Power to the bold;
Heaven to the virtuous.

❧

WEALTH

"In death there is no difference between dying worth a great
sum and dying in debt for a great sum."

❧

SERVICE IS NO INHERITANCE

*Benjamin Franklin Bache, the son of Ben Franklin's daughter
Sarah and her husband Richard, had come back from Geneva in
the winter of 1783 to 1784, to learn printing under Franklin's
direction. Franklin, beginning to realize that his other grandson,
William Temple Franklin, might not able to turn his services to
the public into a later career, explained to Richard Bache in
Philadelphia why "Benny" was being taught a trade. This letter
was written from Passy on November 11, 1784.*

I RECEIVED your letters of the 28th of August and 10th
of September, with the newspapers, by M. Sailly, but they
were very incomplete and broken sets, many being omit-
ted, perhaps the most material: which is disagreeable to
me who wish to be well informed of what is doing among
you. I was glad to receive the good account B—— and
S—— have given of their good treatment of those trifling

correspondents. Your family having passed well through the summer gives me great pleasure. I still hope to see them before I die. Benny continues well, and grows amazingly. He is a very sensible and a very good lad, and I love him much. I had thoughts of bringing him up under his cousin, and fitting him for public business, thinking he might be of service hereafter to his country; but being now convinced that Service is no Inheritance, as the proverb says, I have determined to give him a trade, that he may have something to depend on and not be obliged to ask favours or offices of anybody. And I flatter myself he will make his way good in the world, with God's blessing. He has already begun to learn the business from masters who come to my house, and is very diligent in working and quick in learning. He will write by this opportunity.

I can say nothing certain with respect to my return at present. In the spring I may see clearer. My malady, though it does not permit my using a carriage, is otherwise tolerable. I enjoy the company of my friends, and pass my time as well as can be expected from an exile. My love to Sally and the children, from your affectionate father…

❧

LAST WILL AND TESTAMENT

Franklin put off work on the autobiography and instead (in July 1788) worked on his will. He added a Codicil to it in June 1789. As early as November 18, 1785, he had written to Charles Joseph Mathon de la Cour of Lyons that one of his suggestions "had put it into the head and heart of a citizen to leave two thousand pounds sterling to two American cities who are to lend it in small sums at five per cent to young beginners in business; and the accumulation, after a hundred years, to be laid out in public works of benefit to those cities." In July 1788 Franklin appears to have thought that this two thousand pounds would be best left for making the Schuylkill navigable; in his Codicil he transferred it to the purpose mentioned to Mathon de la Cour.

I, BENJAMIN FRANKLIN, of Philadelphia, printer, late Minister Plenipotentiary from the United States of America to the Court of France, now President of the State of Pennsylvania, do make and declare my last will and testament as follows.

To my son, William Franklin, late Governor of the Jerseys, I give and devise all the lands I hold or have a right to, in the province of Nova Scotia, to hold to him, his heirs, and assigns forever. I also give to him all my books and papers which he has in his possession, and all debts standing against him on my account books, willing that no payment for, nor restitution of, the same be required of him, by my executors. The part he acted against me in the late war, which is of public notoriety, will account for my leaving him no more of an estate he endeavoured to deprive me of.

Having since my return from France demolished the three houses in Market Street, between Third and Fourth Streets, fronting my dwelling-house, and erected two new and larger ones on the ground, and having also erected another house on the lot which formerly was the passage to my dwelling, and also a printing-office between my dwelling anad the front houses; now I do give and devise my said dwelling-house wherein I now live, my said three new houses, my printing-office and the lots of ground thereto belonging; also my small lot and house in Sixth Street, which I bought of the Widow Henmarsh; also my pasture-ground which I have in Hickory Lane, with the buildings thereon; also my house and lot on the north side of Market Street, now occupied by Mary Jacobs, together with two houses and lots behind the same, and fronting on Pewter-Platter Alley; also my lot of ground in Arch Street, opposite the Church burying-ground, with the buildings thereon erected; also all my silver plate, pictures, and household goods, of every kind, now in my said dwelling-house, to my daughter, Sarah Bache, and to her husband, Richard Bache, to hold to them for and during their natural lives, and the life of the longest liver of them. And from and after the decease of the survivor of them, I do give, devise, and bequeth the same to all children already born, or to be born of my said daughter, and to their heirs and assigns forever, as tenants in common, and not as joint tenants.

And if any or either of them shall happen to die under age, and without issue, the part and share of him, her, or them, so dying, shall go to and be equally divided among the survivors or survivor of them. But my intention is that, if any or either of them should happen to die under age, leaving issue, such issue shall inherit the part and share that would have passed to his, her, or their parent, had he, she, or they been living. And as some of my said devisees may, at the death of the survivor of their father or mother, be of age, and others of them under age, so as that all of them may not be of capacity to make division, I in that case request and authorize the judges of the Supreme Court of Judicature of Pennsylvania for the time being, or any three of them, not personally interested, to appoint by writing, under their hands and seals, three honest, intelligent, impartial men to make the said division, and to assign and allot to each of my devisees their respective share, which division, so made and committed to writing under the hands and seals of the said three men, or of any two of them, and confirmed by the said judges, I do hereby declare shall be binding on, and conclusive between, the said devisees.

All the lands near Ohio, and the lots near the centre of Philadelphia, which I lately purchased of the State, I give to my son-in-law, Richard Bache, his heirs and assigns forever; I also give him the bond I have against him, of two thousand one hundred and seventy-two pounds, five shillings, together with the interest that shall or may accrue thereon, and direct the same to be delivered up to him by my executors, can-celled, requesting that, in consideration thereof, he would immediately after my decease manumit and set free his Negro man Bob. I leave to him, also, the money due to me from the State of Virginia for types. I also give to him the bond of William Goddard and his sister, and the counter bond of the late Robert Grace, and the bond and judgement of Francis Childs, if not recovered before my decease, or any other bonds, except the bond due from—Killan, of Delaware State, which I give to my grandson, Benjamin Franklin Bache. I also discharge him, my said son-in-law, from all claim and rent of moneys due to me, on book account or otherwise. I also give him all my musical instruments.

The King of France's picture, set with four hundred and eight diamonds, I give to my daughter, Sarah Bache, requesting, however, that she would not form any of those diamonds into ornaments either for herself or daughters, and thereby introduce or countenance the expensive, vain, and useless fashion of wearing jewels in this country; and those immediately connected with the picture may be preserved with the same.

I give and devise to my dear sister, Jane Mecom, a house and lot I have in Unity Street, Boston, now or late under the care of Mr. Jonathan Williams, to her and to her heirs and assigns forever. I also give her the yearly sum of fifty pounds sterling, during life, to commence at my death, and to be paid to her annually out of the interests or dividends arising on twelve shares which I have since my arrival at Philadelphia purchased in the Bank of North America, and, at her decease, I give the said twelve shares in the bank to my daughter, Sarah Bache, and her husband, Richard Bache. But it is my express will and desire that, after payment of the above fifty pounds sterling annually to my said sister, my said daughter be allowed to apply the residue of the interest or dividends on those shares to her sole and separate use, during the life of my said sister, and afterwards the whole of the interest or dividends thereof as her private pocket money.

I give the right I have to take up three thousand acres of land in the State of Georgia, granted to me by the government of that State, to my grandson, William Temple Franklin, his heirs and assigns forever. I also give to my grandson, William Temple Franklin, the bond and judgment I have against him of four thousand pounds sterling, my right to the same to cease upon the day of his marriage; and if he dies unmarried, my will is, that the same be recovered and divided among my other grandchildren the children of my daughter, Sarah Bache, in such manner and form as I have herein before given to them the other parts of my estate.

The philosophical instruments I have in Philadelphia I give to my ingenious friend, Francis Hopkinson.

To the children, grandchildren, and great grandchildren of my brother, Samuel Franklin, that may be living at the time of my decease, I give fifty pounds sterling, to be equally divided among them. To the children, grandchildren, and great-grandchildren of my sister, Anne Harris, that may be living at the time of my decease, I give fifty pounds sterling, to be equally divided among them. To the children, grandchildren, and great-grandchildren of my brother, James Franklin, that may be living at the time of my decease, I give fifty pounds sterling, to be equally divided among them. To the children, grandchildren, and great-grandchildren of my sister, Lydia Scott, that may be living at the time of my decease, I give fifty pounds sterling, to be equally divided among them.

I give to my grandson, Benjamin Franklin Bache, all the types and printing materials which I now have in

Philadelphia, with the complete letter foundery, which, in the whole, I suppose to be worth near one thousand pounds; but if he should die under age, and without children, then I do order the same to be sold by my executors, the survivors or survivor of them, and the moneys thence arising to be equally divided among all the rest of my said daughter's children, or their representatives, each one on coming of age to take his or her share, and the children of such of them as may die under age to represent, and to take the share and proportion of, the parent so dying, each one to receive his or her part of such share as they come of age.

With regard to my books, those I had in France and those I left in Philadelphia being now assembled together here, and a catalogue made of them, it is my intention to dispose of the same as follows: My "History of the Academy of Sciences," in sixty or seventy volumes quarto, I give to the Philosophical Society of Philadelphia, of which I have the honour to be President. My collection in folio of "Les Arts et les Métiers," I give to the American Philosophical Society, established in New England, of which I am a member. My quarto edition of the same "Arts et Métiers," I give to the Library Company of Philadelphia. Such and so many of my books as I shall mark on the said catalogue with the name of my grandson, Benjamin Franklin Bache, I do hereby give to him; and such and so many of my books as I shall mark on the said catalogue with the name of my grandson, William Bache, I do hereby give to him; and such as shall be marked with the name of Jonathan Williams, I hereby give to my cousin of that name. The residue and remainder of all my books, manuscripts, and papers, I do give to my grandson William Temple Franklin. My share in the Library Company of Philadelphia, I give to my grandson, Benjamin Franklin Bache, confiding that he will permit his brothers and sisters to share in the use of it.

I was born in Boston, New England, and owe my first instructions in literature to the free grammar schools established there. I therefore give one hundred pounds sterling to my executors, to be by them, the survivors or survivor of them, paid over to the managers or directors of the free schools in my native town of Boston, to be by them, or by those person or persons who shall have the superintendence and management of the said schools, put out to interest, and so continued at interest forever, which interest annually shall be laid out in silver medals, and given as honorary rewards annually by the directors of the said free schools belonging to the said town, in such manner as to the discretion of the selectmen of the said town shall seem meet.

Out of the salary that may remain due to me as President of the State, I do give the sum of two thousand pounds to my executors, to be by them, the survivors or survivor of them, paid over to such person or persons as the legislature of this State by an act of Assembly shall appoint to receive the same in trust, to be employed for making the river Schuylkill navigable.

And what money of mine shall, at the time of my decease, remain in the hands of my bankers, Messrs. Ferdinand Grand and Son, at Paris, or Messrs. Smith, Wright, and Gray, of London, I will that, after my debts are paid and deducted, with the money legacies of this my will, the same be divided into four equal parts, two of which I give to my dear daughter, Sarah Bache, one to her son Benjamin, and one to my grandson, William Temple Franklin.

During the number of years I was in business as a stationer, printer, and postmaster, a great many small sums became due for books, advertisements, postage of letters, and other matters, which were not collected when, in 1757, I was sent by the Assembly to England as their agent, and by subsequent appointments continued there till 1775, when on my return, I was immediately engaged in the affairs of Congress, and sent to France in 1776, where I remained nine years, not returning till 1785: and the said debts, not being demanded in such a length of time, are become in a manner obsolete, yet are nevertheless justly due. These, as they are stated in my great folio Ledger E, I bequeath to the contributors to the Pennsylvania Hospital, hoping that those debtors, and the descendants of such as are deceased, who now, as I find, make some difficulty of satisfying such antiquated demands as just debts, may, however, be induced to pay or give them as charity to that excellent institution. I am sensible that much must inevitably be lost, but I hope something considerable may be recovered. It is possible too, that some of the parties charged may have existing old, unsettled accounts against me.

I request my friends, Henry Hill, Esquire, John Jar, Esquire, Francis Hopkinson, Esquire, and Mr. Edward Duffield, of Benfield, in Philadelphia County, to be the executors of this my last will and testament; and I hereby nominate and appoint them for that purpose.

I would have my body buried with as little expense or ceremony as may be. I revoke all former wills by me made, declaring this only to be my last.

In witness thereof, I have hereunto set my hand and seal, this seventeenth day of July, in the year of our Lord one thousand seven hundred and eighty eight.

B. FRANKLIN

Signed, sealed, published, and declared by the above named Benjamin Franklin, for and as his last will and testament, in the presence of us.

ABRAHAM SHOEMAKER,
JOHN JONES,
GEORGE MOORE

CODICIL

I, Benjamin Franklin, in the foregoing or annexed last will and testament named, having further considered the same, do think proper to make and publish the following codicil or addition thereto.

It having long been a fixed political opinion of mine, that in a democratical state there ought to be no offices of profit, for the reasons I had given in an article of my drawing in our Constitution, it was my intention when I accepted the office of president, to devote the appointed salary to some public uses. Accordingly, I had already, before I made my will in July last, given large sums of it to colleges, schools, building of churches, etc.; and in that will I bequeathed two thousand pounds more to the State for the purpose of making the Schuylkill navigable. But understanding since that such a sum will do but little towards accomplishing such a work, and that the project is not likely to he undertaken for many years to come, and having entertained another idea that I hope may be more extensively useful, I do hereby revoke and annul that bequest, and direct that the certificates I have for what remains due to me of that salary be sold, towards raising the sum of two thousand pounds sterling, to be disposed of as I am now about to order.

It has been an opinion, that he who receives an estate from his ancestors is under some kind of obligation to transmit the same to their posterity. This obligation does not lie on me, who never inherited a shilling from any ancestor or relation. I shall, however, if it is not diminished by some accident before my death, leave a considerable estate among my descendants and relations. The above observation is made merely as some apology to my family for making bequests that do not appear to have any immediate relation to their advantage.

I was born in Boston, New England, and owe my first instructions in literature to the free grammar schools established there. I have, therefore, already considered these schools in my will. But I am also under obligations to the State of Massachusetts for having, unasked, appointed me formerly their agent in England, with a handsome salary, which continued some years; and although I accidentally lost in their service, by transmitting Governor Hutchinson's letters, much more than the amount of what they gave me, I do not think that ought in the least to diminish my gratitude.

I have considered that, among artisans, good apprentices are most likely to make good citizens, and, having myself been bred to a manual art, printing, in my native town, and afterwards assisted to set up my business in Philadelphia by kind loans of money from two friends there, which was the foundation of my fortune, and of all the utility in life that may he ascribed to me, I wish to be useful even after my death, if possible, in forming and advancing other young men that may be serviceable to their country in both those towns. To this end, I devote two thousand pounds sterling, of which I give one thousand thereof to the inhabitants of the town of Boston, in Massachusetts, and the other thousand to the inhabitants of the city of Philadelphia, in trust, to and for the uses, intents, and purposes hereinafter mentioned and declared.

The said sum of one thousand pounds sterling, if accepted by the inhabitants of the town of Boston, shall be managed under the direction of the selectmen, united with the ministers of the oldest Episcopalian, Congregational, and Presbyterian churches in that town, who are to let out the sum upon interest at five per cent, per annum, to such young married artificers, under the age of twenty five years, as have served an apprenticeship in the said town, and faithfully fulfilled the duties required in their indentures, so as to obtain a good moral character from at least two respectable citizens, who are willing to become their sureties, in a bond with the applicants, for the repayment of the moneys so lent, with interest, according to the terms hereinafter prescribed; all which bonds are to be taken for Spanish milled dollars, or the value thereof in current gold coin; and the managers shall keep a bound book or books, wherein shall be entered the names of those who shall apply for and receive the benefits of this institution, and of their sureties, together with the sums lent, the dates, and other necessary and proper records respecting the business and concerns of this institution. And as these loans are intended to assist young married artificers in setting up their business, they are to be proportioned by the discretion of the managers, so as not to exceed sixty pounds sterling to one person, nor to be less than fifteen pounds; and if the number of appliers so entitled should be so large as that the sum will not suffice to afford to each as much as might otherwise not be improper, the proportion to each shall be diminished so as to afford to every one some assistance. These aids, may therefore, be small at first, but, as the capital increases by the accumulated interest, they will be more ample. And in order to serve as many as possible in their turn, as well as to make the repayment of the principal borrowed more easy, each borrower shall be obliged to pay, with the yearly interest, one tenth part of the principal, which sums of principal and interest, so paid in, shall be again let out to fresh borrowers.

And, as it is presumed that there will always be found in Boston virtuous and benevolent citizens, willing to bestow a part of their time in doing good to the rising generation, by superintending and managing this institution gratis, it is hoped that no part of the money will at any time be dead, or be diverted to other purposes, but be continually augmenting by the interest; in which case there may, in time, be more than the occasions in Boston shall require, and then some may be spared to the neighbouring or other towns in the said State of Massachusetts, who may desire to have it; such towns engaging to pay punctually the interest and the portions of the principal, annually, to the inhabitants of the town of Boston.

If this plan is executed, and succeeds as projected without interruption for one hundred years, the sum will then be one hundred and thirty-one thousand pounds; of which I would have the managers of the donation to the town of Boston then lay out, at their discretion, one hundred thousand pounds in public works, which may be judged of most general utility to the inhabitants, such as fortifications, bridges, aqueducts, public buildings, baths, pavements, or whatever may make living in the town more convenient to its people, and render it more agreeable to strangers resorting thither for health or a temporary residence, The remaining thirty one thousand pounds I would have continued to be let out on interest, in the manner above directed, for another hundred years, as I hope it will have been found that the institution has had a good effect on the conduct of youth, and been of service to many worthy characters and useful citizens. At the end of this second term, if no unfortunate accident has prevented the operation, the sum will be four millions and sixty one thousand pounds sterling, of which I leave one million sixty one thousand pounds to the disposition of the inhabitants of the town of Boston, and three millions to the disposition of the government of the State, not presuming to carry my views farther.

All the directions herein given, respecting the disposition and management of the donation to the inhabitants of Boston, I would have observed respecting that to the inhabitants of Philadelphia, only, as Philadelphia is incorporated, I request the corporation of that city to undertake the management agreeably to the said directions; and I do hereby vest them with full and ample powers for that purpose. And, having considered that covering ground with buildings and pavements, which carry off most of the rain and prevent its soaking into the earth and renewing and purifying the springs, whence the water of wells must gradually grow worse, and in time be unfit for use, as I find has happened in all old cities, I recommend that at the end of the first hundred years, if not done before, the corporation of the city employ a part of the hundred thousand pounds in bringing, by pipes, the water of Wissahickon Creek into the town, so as to supply the inhabitants, which I apprehend may be done without great difficulty, the level of the creek being much above that of the city, and may be made higher by a dam. I also recommend making the Schuylkill completely navigable. At the end of the second hundred years, I would have the disposition of the four million and sixty one thousand pounds divided between the inhabitants of the city of Philadelphia and the government of Pennsylvania, in the same manner as herein directed with respect to that of the inhabitants of Boston and the government of Massachusetts.

It is my desire that this institution should take place and begin to operate within one year after my decease, for which purpose due notice should be publicly given previous to the expiration of that year, that those for whose benefit this establishment is intended may make their respective applications. And I hereby direct my executors, the survivors or survivor of them, within six months after my decease, to pay over the said sum of two thousand pounds sterling to such persons as shall be duly appointed by the selectmen of Boston and the corporation of Philadelphia, to receive and take charge of their respective sums, of one thousand pounds each, for the purposes aforesaid.

Considering the accidents to which all human affairs and projects are subject in such a length of time, I have, perhaps, too much flattered myself with a vain fancy that these dispositions, if carried into execution, will be continued without interruption and have the effects proposed. I hope, however, that if the inhabitants of the two cities should not think fit to undertake the execution, they will, at least, accept the offer of these donations as a mark of my good will, a token of my gratitude, and a testimony of my earnest desire to be useful to them after my departure. I wish, indeed, that they may both undertake to endeavour the execution of the project, because I think that, though unforeseen difficulties may arise, expedients will be found to remove them, and the scheme be found practicable. If one of them accepts the money, with the conditions, and the other refuses, my will then is, that both sums be given to the Inhabitants of the city accepting, the whole to be applied to the same purposes, and under the same regulations directed for the separate parts; and, if both refuse, the money of course remains in the mass of my estate, and is to be disposed of therewith according to my will made the seventeenth day of July, 1788.

I wish to be buried by the side of my wife, if it may be, and that a marble stone, to be made by Chambers, six feet long, four feet wide, plain, with only a small moulding round the upper edge, and this inscription:

BENJAM1N AND DEBORAH FRANKLIN 178-
to be placed over us both.

My fine crab tree walking stick, with a gold head curiously wrought in the form of the cap of liberty, I give to my friend, and the friend of mankind, General Washington. If it were a sceptre, he has merited it, and would become it. It was a present to me from that excellent woman, Madame de Forbach, the Dowager Duchess of Deux Ponts, connected with some verses which should go with it.

I give my gold watch to my son in law, Richard Bache, and also the gold watch chain of the Thirteen United States, which I have not yet worn. My time piece, that stands in my library, I give to my grandson, William Temple Franklin. I give him also my Chinese gong. To my dear old friend, Mrs. Mary Hewson, I give one of my silver tankards marked for her use during her life, and after her decease I give it to her daughter Eliza. I give to her son, William Hewson, who is my godson, my new quarto Bible, Oxford edition, to be for his family Bible, and also the botanic description of the plants in the Emperor's garden at Vienna, in folio, with coloured cuts. And to her son, Thomas Hewson, I give a set of Spectators, Tatters, and Guardians handsomely bound.

There is an error in my will, where the bond of William Temple Franklin is mentioned as being four thousand pounds sterling, whereas it is but for three thousand five hundred pounds.

I give to my executors, to be divided equally among those that act, the sum of sixty pounds sterling, as some compensation for their trouble in the execution of my will; and I request my friend, Mr. Duffield, to accept moreover my French wayweiser, a piece of clockwork in brass, to be fixed to the wheel of any carriage; and that my friend, Mr. Hill, may also accept my silver cream-pot, formerly given to me by the good Doctor Fothergill, with the motto, Keep bright the chain. My reflecting telescope, made by Short, which was formerly Mr. Canton's, I give to my friend, Mr. David Rittenhouse, for the use of his observatory.

My picture, drawn by Martin in 1767, I give to the Supreme Executive Council of Pennsylvania, if they shall be pleased to do me the honour of accepting it and placing it in their chamber.

Since my will was made I have bought some more city lots, near the centre part of the estate of Joseph Dean. I would have them go with the other lots, disposed of in my will, and I do give the same to my son-in-law, Richard Bache, to his heirs and assigns forever.

In addition to the annuity left to my sister in my will, of fifty pounds sterling during her life, I now add thereto ten pounds sterling more, in order to make the sum sixty pounds.

I give twenty guineas to my good friend and physician, Dr. John Jones.

With regard to the separate bequests made to my daughter Sarah in my will, my intention is, that the same shall be for her sole and separate use, notwithstanding her coverture, or whether she be covert or sole; and I do give my executors so much right and power therein as may be necessary to render my intention effectual in that respect only. This provision for my daughter is not made out of any disrespect I have for her husband.

And lastly, it is my desire that this, my present codicil, be annexed to, and considered as part of, my last will and testament to all intents and purposes.

In witness whereof, I have hereunto set my hand and seal this twenty-third day of June, Anno Domini one thousand seven hundred and eighty-nine.

B. Franklin

Signed, sealed, published, and declared by the above-named Benjamin Franklin to be a codicil to his last will and testament, in the presence of us.

Francis Bailey,
Thomas Lang,
Abraham Shoemaker.

PART VI

Poor Richard's Way to Wealth

Father *Abraham* in his STUDY.

To Failings mild, but zealous for Desert;
The clearest Head, and the sincerest Heart.

Good-Nature, Wit, and *Judgment* round him wait;
And thus he fits *inthron'd* in *Classick-State*:

He's rarely *warm* in } Censure or in Praise;

Few Men desire our } *Passions* either Ways.

THE SHADE of Him who Counsel can bestow,
Still pleas'd to teach, and yet not proud to know;
Unbias'd or by Favour or by Spite;
Nor dully prepossess'd, nor blindly right;
Thô learn'd, well-bred; and, thô well-bred, sincere;
Modestly bold, and humanely severe;
Who to a Friend his Faults can sweetly show,
And gladly praise the Merit of a Foe.
Here, there he sits, his chearful Aid to lend;
A firm, unshaken, uncorrupted Friend,
Averse alike to flatter or offend. }

Printed by Benjamin Mecom, *at the* New
Printing-Office, *(near the* TOWN-HOUSE, *in* Boston) *where*
BOOKS *are Sold, and* PRINTING-WORK *done, Cheap.*

POOR RICHARD'S WAY TO WEALTH

Franklin published Poor Richard's Almanack *with two goals in mind: the making of money and the promotion of virtue. The almanac ran for twenty-five years (1732—1757) and became America's first great humor classic with characters like Richard Saunders and his nagging wife Bridget. These characters seemed naive, yet were quite sharp.*

In July 1757, Franklin wrote the preface to what would be his final edition of Poor Richard's Almanack. *In it he invented the character Father Abraham, who gives a speech that strings together all of the best and most famous maxims that Poor Richard had sprinkled in the margins of his almanacs over the years. Poor Richard, portrayed standing in the back of the crowd, reports at the end, "The people heard it, and approved the doctrine—and immediately practiced the contrary."*

Father Abraham's speech was soon published as "The Way to Wealth," becoming an instant classic. Within forty years, it was reprinted in 145 editions and seven languages.

Advertisement.

This famous SPEECH *most certainly does hit*
The happy Point where Wisdom *joins with* Wit.

AT the first Appearance of this humorous and instructive Production, several Gentlemen of approved *Taste* were struck with the Design and Beauty of it, and therefore desired to know the *Parent's* Name.---Father *Abraham's* Speech is the comely *Off-spring* of that *Frank lyn-cean* GENIUS who is the Author of a Pamphlet intitled *The Interest of* Great Britain *considered*; and of the following Quotations from the Additions to said Pamphlet, *viz.*

" The Legislator that makes effectual Laws for promoting of Trade, increasing Employment, improving Land by more or better Tillage, providing more Food by Fisheries, securing Property, &c. and the Man that invents new Trades, Arts, or Manufactures, or new Improvements in Husbandry, may be properly called FATHERS *of their Nation,* as they are the Cause of the Generation of Multitudes, by the Encouragement they afford to Marriage."

" The greater the common fashionable Expence of any Rank of People, the more cautious they are of Marriage : Therefore Luxury should never be suffered to become common."

" The great Increase of Offspring in particular Families, is not always owing to greater Fecundity of Nature, but sometimes to Examples of Industry in the Heads, and industrious Education ; by which the Children are enabled to provide better for themselves ; and their marrying early is encouraged from the Prospect of good Subsistence."

" If there be a Sect therefore, in our Nation, that regard Frugality and Industry as religious Duties, and educate their Children therein, more than others commonly do ; such Sect must consequently increase more by natural Generation, than any other Sect in *Britain.*"

FATHER
Abraham's
SPEECH

To a great Number of People, at a Vendue of Merchant-Goods ;

Introduced to The PUBLICK

By Poor *RICHARD*,

(A famous Pennsylvanian Conjurer and Almanack-Maker)

In Anſwer to the following Queſtions.

Pray, Father *Abraham*, what think you of the Times ? Won't theſe heavy Taxes quite ruin the Country ? How ſhall we be ever able to pay them ? What would you adviſe us to ?

Printed and Sold by Benjamin Mecom, *at the* New Printing-Office, *near the* Town-Houſe, *in* BOSTON.

105

Father *Abraham*'s Speech, introduced by *Poor Richard*, viz.

Courteous Reader,

I Have heard that Nothing gives an Author so great Pleasure, as to find his Works respectfully quoted by other learned Authors. This Pleasure I have seldom enjoyed; for though I have been, if I may say it without Vanity, an *eminent Author* of Almanacks annually now a full Quarter of a Century, my Brother-Authors in the same Way, for what Reason I know not, have ever been very sparing in their Applauses; and no other Author has taken the least Notice of me, so that did not my Writings produce me some solid *Pudding*, the great Deficiency of *Praise* would have quite discouraged me.

I concluded at length, that the People were the best Judges of my Merit; for they buy my Works; and besides, in my Rambles, where I am not personally known, I have frequently heard one or other of my Adages repeated, with *as Poor Richard says*, at the End on't. This gave me some Satisfaction, as it shewed not only that my Instructions were regarded, but discovered likewise some Respect for my Authority; and I own that, to encourage the Practice of remembering and repeating those wise Sentences, I have sometimes *quoted myself*, with great Gravity.

Father Abraham's Speech

COURTEOUS READER,

I Have heard that Nothing gives an author so great Pleasure, as to find his Works respectfully quoted by other learned Authors. This Pleasure I have seldom enjoyed; for though I have been, if I may say it without Vanity, an *eminent Author* of Almanacks annually now a full Quarter of a Century, my Brother-Authors in the same Way, for what Reason I know not, have ever been very sparing in their Applauses; and no other Author has taken the least Notice of me, so that did not my Writings produce me some solid *Pudding*, the great Deficiency of *Praise* would have quite discouraged me.

I concluded at length, that the People were the best Judges of my Merit; for they buy my Works; and besides, in my Rambles, where I am not personally known, I have frequently heard one or other of my Adages repeated, with *as Poor Richard says*, at the End of it. This gave me some Satisfaction, as it showed not only that my Instructions were regarded, but discovered likewise some Respect for my Authority; and I own that, to encourage the practice of remembering and repeating those wise Sentences, I have sometimes *quoted myself*, with great Gravity.

Father *Abraham*'s Speech.

Judge then how much I muſt have been gratified by an Incident I am going to relate to you. I ſtopt my Horſe lately where a great Number of People were collected at a Vendue of Merchant Goods. The Hour of Sale not being come, they were converſing on the Badneſs of the Times, and one of the Company call'd to a plain clean old Man, with white Locks, *Pray, Father* Abraham, *what think you of the Times? Won't theſe heavy Taxes quite ruin the Country? How ſhall we be ever able to pay them? What would you adviſe us to?* --- Father *Abraham* ſtood up and reply'd, If you'd have my Advice, I'll give it you in ſhort, for *A Word to the Wiſe is enough*, and *Many Words won't fill a Buſhel*, as *Poor Richard* ſays. They joined in deſiring him to ſpeak his Mind, and gathering round him, he proceeded as follows.

" *Friends and Neighbours,*
THE Taxes are indeed very heavy, and if thoſe laid on by the Goverment were the only Ones we had to pay, we might more eaſily diſcharge them ; but we have many others, and much more grievous to ſome of us. We are taxed twice as much by our *Idleneſs*, three times as much by our *Pride*, and four times as much by our *Folly*, and from theſe Taxes the Commiſſioners cannot eaſe or deliver us by allowing an Abatement. However, let us hearken to good Advice, and ſomething may be done for us. *God helps them that help themſelves*, as *Poor Richard* ſays, in his Almanack of 1733.

108

Father Abraham's Speech

Judge then how much I must have been gratified by an Incident I am going to relate to you. I stopped my Horse lately where a great Number of People were collected at a Vendue of Merchant Goods. The Hour of Sale not being come, they were conversing on the Badness of the Times, and one of the Company called to a plain clean old Man, with white Locks, *Pray, Father* Abraham, *what think you of the Times? Won't these heavy Taxes quite ruin the Country? How shall we be ever able to pay them? What would you advise us to do?* Father *Abraham* stood up and replied, If you'd have my Advice, I'll give it you in short, for *A Word to the Wise is enough*, and *Many Words won't fill a Bushel*, as *Poor Richard* says. They joined in desiring him to speak his Mind, and gathering round him, he proceeded as follows.

"*Friends and Neighbors,*

THE Taxes are indeed very heavy, and if those laid on by the Government were the only Ones we had to pay, we might more easily discharge them; but we have many others, and much more grievous to some of us. We are taxed twice as much by our *Idleness*, three times as much by our *Pride*, and four times as much by our *Folly*, and from these Taxes the Commissioners cannot ease or deliver us by allowing an Abatement. However let us hearken to good Advice, and something may be done for us. *God helps them that help themselves*, as *Poor Richard* says, in his Almanack of 1733.

Father *Abraham*'s Speech.

It would be thought a hard Goverment that fhould tax its People one tenth Part of their *Time*, to be employed in its Service. But *Idlene/s* taxes many of us much more, if we reckon all that is fpent in abfolute *Sloth*, or doing of Nothing, with that which is fpent in idle Employments or Amufements, that amount to Nothing. *Sloth*, by bringing on Difeafes, abfolutely fhortens Life. *Sloth, like Ruft, confumes fafter than Labour wears, while the ufed Key is always bright*, as *Poor Richard* fays. But *Doft thou love Life? then do not fquander Time, for that's the Stuff Life is made of*, as *Poor Richard* fays: How much more than is neceffary do we fpend in Sleep! forgetting that *The fleeping Fox catches no Poultry*, and that *There will be fleeping enough in the Grave*, as *Poor Richard* fays. If Time be of all Things the moft precious, *wafting Time* muft be, as *Poor Richard* fays, *The greateft Prodigality*, fince, as he elfewere tells us, *Loft Time is never found again*; and what we call *Time enough, always proves little enough*. Let us then up and be doing, and doing to the Purpofe; fo by Diligence fhall we do more with lefs Perplexity. *Sloth makes all Things difficult, but Induftry all eafy*, as *Poor Richard* fays; and *He that rifeth late, muft trot all Day, and fhall fcarce overtake his Bufine/s at Night*; while *Lazine/s travels fo flowly, that Poverty foon overtakes him*, as we read in *Poor Richard*; who adds *Drive thy Bufine/s, let not that drive thee*; and *Early to Bed, and early to rife, makes a Man healthy, wealthy and wife*.

It would be thought a hard Government that should tax its People one tenth Part of their *Time*, to be employed in its Service. But *Idleness* taxes many of us much more, if we reckon all that is spent in absolute *Sloth*, or doing of Nothing, with that which is spent in idle Employments or Amusements, that amount to nothing. *Sloth*, by bringing on Diseases, absolutely shortens Life. *Sloth, like Rust, consumes faster than Labor wears, while the used Key is always bright*, as *Poor Richard* says. But *Dost thou love Life? then do not squander Time, for that's the Stuff Life is made of*, as *Poor Richard* says: How much more than is necessary do we spend in Sleep! forgetting that *The sleeping Fox catches no Poultry*, and that *There will be sleeping enough in the Grave*, as *Poor Richard* says. If Time be of all Things the most precious, *wasting Time* must be, as *Poor Richard* says, *The greatest Prodigality*, since, as he elsewhere tells us, *Lost Time is never found again*, and what we call *Time enough, always proves little enough*. Let us then up and be doing, and doing to the Purpose; so by Diligence shall we do more with less Perplexity. *Sloth makes all Things difficult, but Industry all easy*, as *Poor Richard* says; and *He that riseth late, must trot all Day, and shall scarce overtake his Business at Night;* while *Laziness travels so slowly, that Poverty soon overtakes him*, as we read in *Poor Richard*; who adds, *Drive thy Business, let not that drive thee; and Early to Bed,* and *early to rise, makes a Man healthy, wealthy and wise.*

111

Father *Abraham*'s Speech.

So what fignifies *wifhing* and *hoping* for better Times. We may make thefe Times better if we beftir ourfelves. *Induftry need not wifh*, as *Poor Richard* fays, and *He that lives upon Hope will die fafting*. *There are no Gains without Pains* ; then *Help Hands, for I have no Lands*, or if I have, they are fmartly taxed. And, as *Poor Richard* likewife obferves, *He that hath a Trade hath an Eftate*, and *He that hath a Calling hath an Office of Profit and Honour* ; but then the *Trade* muft be worked at, and the *Calling* well followed, or neither the *Eftate*, nor the *Office*, will enable us to pay our Taxes. If we are induftrious we fhall never ftarve ; for, as *Poor Richard* fays, *At the working Man's Houfe* Hunger *looks in, but dares not enter*. Nor will the Bailiff or the Conftable enter, for *Induftry pays Debts, while Defpair encreafeth them*, fays *Poor Richard*. What though you have found no Treafure, nor has any rich Relation left you a Legacy, *Diligence is the Mother of Good-luck*, as *Poor Richard* fays, and *God gives all Things to Induftry* : Then *Plough deep, while Sluggards fleep, and you fhall have Corn to fell and to keep*, fays *Poor Dick*. Work while it is called To-day, for you know not how much you may be hindered To-morrow, which makes *Poor Richard* fay *One To-day is worth two To-morrows* ; and far-ther, *Have you fomewhat to do To-morrow ? do it To-day*. If you were a Servant, would you not be afhamed that a good Mafter fhould catch you idle ? Are you then your own Mafter ? *Be afhamed to catch*

So what signifies *wishing* and *hoping* for better Times. We may make these Times better if we bestir ourselves. *Industry need not wish*, as *Poor Richard* says, and *He that lives upon Hope will die fasting. There are no Gains, without Pains;* then *Help Hands for l have no Lands*, or if I have, they are smartly taxed. And, as *Poor Richard* likewise observes, *He that hath a Trade hath an Estate,* and *he that hath a Calling hath an Office of Profit and Honor*; but then the *Trade* must be worked at, and the *Calling* well followed, or neither the *Estate*, nor the *Office*, will enable us to pay our Taxes. If we are industrious we shall never starve; for, as *Poor Richard* says, *At the working Man's House* Hunger *looks in, but dares not enter*. Nor will the Bailiff or the Constable enter, for *Industry pays Debts, while Despair increaseth them*, says *Poor Richard*. What though you have found no Treasure, nor has any rich Relation left you a Legacy, *Diligence is the Mother of Good-luck,* as *Poor Richard* says, and *God gives all Things to Industry*: Then *Plough deep, while Sluggards sleep, and you shall have Corn to sell and to keep*, says *Poor Dick*. Work while it is called Today, for you know not how much you may be hindered Tomorrow, which makes *Poor Richard* say, *One Today is worth two Tomorrows*; and farther, *Have you somewhat to do Tomorrow? do it Today*. If you were a Servant, would you not be ashamed that a good Master should catch you idle? Are you then your own Master? *Be ashamed to catch*

Father *Abraham's* Speech.

yourself idle, as *Poor Dick* fays. When there is fo much to be done for your Self, your Family, your Country, and your gracious King, be up by Peep of Day : *Let not the Sun look down and fay*, IN-GLORIOUS HERE HE LIES. Handle your Tools without Mittens ; remember that *The Cat in Gloves catches no Mice*, as *Poor Richard* fays. 'Tis true, there is much to be done, and perhaps you are weak-handed, but flick to it fteadily, and you will fee great Effects, for *Conftant Dropping wears away Stones*, and *By Diligence and Patience the Moufe ate in two the Cable* ; and *Little Strokes fell great Oaks*, as *Poor Richard* fays in his Almanack, the Year I cannot juft now remember.

Methinks I hear fome of you fay, *Muft a Man afford himfelf no Leifure ?* I will tell thee, my Friends, what *Poor Richard* fays. *Employ thy Time well if thou meaneft to gain Leifure* ; and, *Since thou art not fure of a Minute, throw not away an Hour.* Leifure is Time for doing fomething ufeful ; this Leifure the diligent Man will obtain, but the lazy Man never ; fo that, as *Poor Richard* fays, *A Life of Leifure and a Life of Lazinefs are two Things.* Do you imagine that Sloth will afford you more Comfort than Labour ? No ; for, as *Poor Richard* fays, *Trouble fprings from Idlenefs, and grievous Toil from needlefs Eafe. Many without Labour would live by their* WITS *only, but they break for want of Stock.* Whereas Induftry gives Comfort, and Plenty, and Refpect. *Fly Pleafures and they'll follow you.* ---

yourself idle, as *Poor Dick* says. When there is so much to be done for Yourself, your Family, your Country, and your gracious King, be up by Peep of Day: *Let not the Sun look down and say*, INGLORIOUS HERE HE LIES. Handle your Tools without Mittens; remember that *The Cat in Gloves catches no Mice*, as *Poor Richard* says. 'Tis true, there is much to be done, and perhaps you are weakhanded, but stick to it steadily, and you will see great Effects, for *Constant Dropping wears away Stones*, and *By Diligence and Patience the Mouse ate in two the Cable*; and *Little Strokes fell great Oaks*, as *Poor Richard* says in his Almanack, the Year I cannot just now remember.

Methinks I hear some of you say, *Must a Man afford himself no Leisure?* I will tell thee, my Friends, what *Poor Richard* says. *Employ thy Time well if thou meanest to gain Leisure*; and, *Since thou art not sure of a Minute, throw not away an hour.* Leisure is Time for doing something useful; this Leisure the diligent Man will obtain, but the lazy Man never; so that, as *Poor Richard* says, *A Life of Leisure and a Life of Laziness are two Things.* Do you imagine that Sloth will afford you more Comfort than Labor? No; for, as *Poor Richard* says, *Trouble Springs from Idleness, and grievous Toil from needless Ease. Many without Labor would live by their* WITS *only, but they break for want of Stock.* Whereas Industry gives Comfort, and Plenty, and Respect. *Fly Pleasures, and they'll follow you.*—

Father *Abraham*'s Speech.

The diligent Spinner has a large Shift ; and *Now I have a Sheep and a Cow, every Body bids me Good-Morrow* ; all which is well said by *Poor Richard.*

But with our Industry, we must likewise be *steady settled* and *careful,* and oversee our own Affairs *with our own Eyes,* and not trust too much to others ; for, as *Poor Richard* says.

> *I never saw an oft removed Tree,*
> *Nor yet an oft removed Family,*
> *That throve so well as those that settled be.*

And again, *Three-Removes is as bad as a Fire* ; and again *Keep thy Shop, and thy Shop will keep thee* ; and again, *If you would have your Business done, go* ; *if not, send.* And again,

> *He that by the Plough would thrive,*
> *Himself must either hold or drive.*

And again, *The Eye of a Master will do more Work than both his Hands* ; and again, *Want of Care does us more Damage than want of Knowledge* ; and again, *Not to oversee Workmen is to leave them your Purse open.* Trusting too much to others Care is the Ruin of many ; for as the *Almanack* says, *In the Affairs of this World, Men are saved, not by Faith, but by the Want of it* ; but a Man's own Care is profitable ; for, saith *Poor Dick, Learning is to the Studious,* and *Riches to the Careful,* as well as *Power to the Bold,* and *Heaven to the Virtuous.* And farther, *If you would have a faithful Servant, and one that you like,----serve your Self.* And again, he adviseth to Circumspection and

116

Father Abraham's Speech

The diligent Spinner has a large Shift, and *Now I have a Sheep and a Cow, Everybody bids me Good Morrow;* all which is well said by *Poor Richard.*

But with our Industry, we must likewise be *Steady Settled* and *careful,* and oversee our own Affairs *with our own Eyes,* and not trust too much to others; for, as *Poor Richard* says,

> *I never Saw an oft removed Tree,*
> *Nor yet an oft removed Family,*
> *That throve so well as those that Settled be.*

And again, *Three removes is as bad as a Fire*; and again, *Keep the Shop, and thy Shop will keep thee*; and again, *If you would have your Business done; go; if not, send.* And again,

> *He that by the Plough would thrive,*
> *Himself must either hold or drive.*

And again, *The Eye of a Master will do more Work than both his Hands*; and again, *Want of Care does us more Damage than want of Knowledge*; and again, *Not to oversee Workmen is to leave them your Purse open.* Trusting too much to others Care is the Ruin of many; for, as the *Almanack* says, *In the Affairs of this World Men are Saved, not by Faith, but by the Want of it*; but a Man's own Care is profitable; for, faith *Poor Dick, Learning is to the Studious,* and *Riches to the Careful,* as well as *Power to the Bold,* and *Heaven to the Virtuous.* And farther, *If you would have a faithful Servant,* and one that you like,—serve yourself. And again, he adviseth to Circumspection and

Father *Abraham*'s Speech.

Care, even in the fmalleſt Matters, becauſe ſometimes *A little Neglect may breed great Miſchief* ; adding, *For want of a Nail the Shoe was loſt* ; *for want of a Shoe the Horſe was loſt* ; *and for want of a Horſe the Rider was loſt*, being overtaken and ſlain by the Enemy, all for want of Care about a Horſe-ſhoe Nail.

So much for Induſtry, my Friends, and Attention to one's own Buſineſs ; but to theſe we muſt add *Frugality*, if we would make our *Induſtry* more certainly ſucceſsful. A Man may, if he knows not how to ſave as he gets, *keep his Noſe all his Life to the Grindſtone*, and die not worth a *Groat* at laſt. *A fat Kitchen makes a lean Will*, as *Poor Richard* ſays ; and,
Many Eſtates are ſpent in the Getting,
Since Women for Tea forſook Spinning and Knitting,
And Men for Punch forſook Hewing and Splitting.
If you would be wealthy, ſays he in another Almanack, *think of Saving, as well as of Getting* : *The* Indies *have not made* Spain *rich becauſe her* Outgoes *are greater than her* Incomes. Away then with your expenſive Follies, and you will not have ſo much Cauſe to complain of hard Times, heavy Taxes, and chargeable Famlies ; for, as *Poor Dick* ſays,
Women and Wine, Game and Deceit,
Make the Wealth ſmall, and the Wants great.
And farther, *What maintains one Vice, would bring up two Children.* You may think, perhaps, that a

Care, even in the smallest Matters, because sometimes *A little Neglect may breed great Mischief;* adding, *For want of a Nail the Shoe was lost; for want of a Shoe the Horse was lost; and for want of a Horse the Rider was lost,* being overtaken and slain by the Enemy, all for want of Care about a Horse-shoe Nail.

So much for Industry, my Friends, and Attention to one's own Business; but to these we must add *Frugality*, if we would make our Industry more certainly successful. A Man may, if he knows not how to save as he gets, *keep his Nose all his Life to the Grindstone*, and die not worth a *Groat* at last. *A fat Kitchen makes a lean Will,* as *Poor Richard* says; and,

> *Many Estates are Spent in the Getting,*
> *Since Women for Tea forsook Spinning and Knitting, And Men for Punch forsook Hewing and Splitting.*

If you would be wealthy, says he, in another Almanack, *think of Saving as well as of Getting: The* Indies *have not made* Spain *rich because her* Outgoes *are greater than her* Incomes. Away then with your expensive Follies, and you will not have so much Cause to complain of hard Times, heavy Taxes, and chargeable Families; for, as *Poor Dick* says,

> *Women and Wine, Game and Deceit,*
> *Make the Wealth small, and the Wants great.* And farther, *What maintains one Vice, would bring up two Children.* You may think, perhaps, that a

Father *Abraham*'s Speech.

little Tea, or a *little* Punch now and then, Diet a *little* more coſtly, Clothes a *little* finer, and a *little* Entertainment, now and then, can be no *great* Matter; but remember what *Poor Richard* ſays, *Many a Little makes a Mickle*; and farther, *Beware of little Expences. A ſmall Leak will ſink a great Ship.* And again, *Who Dainties love, ſhall Beggars prove.* And moreover, *Fools make Feaſts and wiſe Men eat them.*

Here you are all got together at this Vendue of *Fineries* and *Knicknacks.* You call them *Goods,* but if you do not take Care, they will prove *Evils* to ſome of you. You expect they will be ſold *cheap,* and perhaps they may for leſs than they coſt; but if you have no Occaſion for them, they muſt be *dear* to you. Remember what *Poor Richard* ſays, *Buy what thou haſt no Need of, and ere long thou ſhalt ſell thy Neceſſaries.* And again, *At a great Pennyworth Pauſe a While.* : He means, that perhaps the Cheapneſs is *apparent* only, and not *real*; or the Bargain, by ſtraitning thee in thy Buſineſs, may do thee more Harm than Good. For in another Place he ſays *Many have been ruined by buying good Pennyworths.* Again *Poor Richard* ſays, *'Tis fooliſh to lay out Money in a Purchaſe of Repentance*; and yet this Folly is practiſed every Day at Vendues, for want of minding the Almanack. *Wiſe Men,* as *Poor Dick* ſays, *learn by others Harms, Fools ſcarcely by their own*; but *Felix quem faciunt aliena Pericula cautum.* Many a One, for the Sake of Finery on the Back, have gone *little* Tea, or a *little* Punch now and then, Diet a *little* more costly, Clothes a *little* finer, and a *little* Entertainment, now and then, can be no *great* Matter; but remember what *Poor Richard* says, *Many* a Little *makes a Mickle*; and farther, *Beware of little Expenses. A small Leak will sink a great Ship.* And again, *Who Dainties love, shall Beggars Prove.* And moreover, *Fools make Feasts, and wise Men eat them.*

Here you are all got together at this vendue of *Fineries* and *Knickknacks.* You call them *Goods*, but if you do not take Care, they will prove *Evils* to some of you. You expect they will be sold *cheap*, and perhaps they may for less than they cost; but if you have no Occasion for them, they must be *dear* to you. Remember what *Poor Richard* says, *Buy what thou hast no Need of, and ere long thou shalt sell thy Necessaries.* And again, *At a great Pennyworth Pause a While*: He means, that perhaps the Cheapness is *apparent* only, and not *real*; or the Bargain, by straitening thee in thy Business, may do thee more Harm than Good. For in another Place he says *Many have been ruined by buying good Pennyworths.* Again, *Poor Richard* says, *'Tis foolish to lay out Money in a Purchase of Repentance*; and yet this Folly is practiced every Day at Vendues, for want of minding the Almanack. *Wise Men*, as *Poor Dick* says, *learn by others' Harms, Fools scarcely by their own*; but *Felix quem faciunt aliena pericula cautum.* Many a One, for the Sake of Finery on the Back, have gone

Father *Abraham*'s Speech.

with a hungry Belly, and half ftarved their Families. *Silks and Sattins, Scarlet and Velvets* (as *Poor Richard* fays) *put out the Kitchen Fire*. Thefe are not the *Neceffaries* of Life, they can fcarcely be called the *Conveniencies*; and yet only becaufe they look pretty, how many *want* to *have* them. The *artificial* Wants of Mankind thus become more numerous than the *natural*; and, as *Poor Dick* fays, *For one* poor *Perfon, there are an hundred* indigent. By thefe, and other Extravagancies, the Genteel are reduced to Poverty, and forced to borrow of thofe whom they formerly defpifed, but who, through *Induftry* and *Frugality*, have maintained their Standing; in which Cafe it appears plainly, that *A Ploughman on his Legs is higher than a Gentleman on his Knees,* as *Poor Richard* fays. Perhaps they have had a fmall Eftate left them, which they knew not the Getting of; they think *'tis Day and will never be Night*; that a little to be fpent out of *fo much,* is not worth minding; (*A Child and a Fool,* as *Poor Richard* fays, *imagine* Twenty Shillings *and Twenty Years can never be fpent*) but, *Always taking out of the Meal-Tub and never putting in foon comes to the Bottom*; then, as *Poor Dick* fays, *When the Well's dry they know the Worth of Water*. But this they might have known before, if they had taken his Advice. *If you would know the Value of Money, go and try to borrow fome*; for, *He that goes a borrow-*

with a hungry Belly, and half starved their Families; *Silks and Satins, Scarlet and Velvets* (as *Poor Richard* says) *put out the Kitchen Fire.* These are not the *Necessaries* of Life, they can scarcely be called the *Conveniencies*; and yet only because they look pretty, how many *want* to *have* them. The *artificial* Wants of Mankind thus become more numerous than the *natural*; and, as *Poor Dick* says, *For one poor Person, there are an hundred* indigent. By these, and other Extravagancies, the Genteel are reduced to Poverty, and forced to borrow of those whom they formerly despised, but who, through *Industry* and *Frugality*, have maintained their Standing; in which Case it appears plainly, that *A Ploughman on his Legs is higher than a Gentleman on his Knees*, as *Poor Richard* says. Perhaps they have had a small Estate left them, which they knew not the Getting of; they think *'tis Day and will never be Night*; that a little to be spent out of *so much*, is not worth minding; (*A Child and a Fool*, as *Poor Richard* says, *imagine* Twenty Shillings *and Twenty Years can never be spent*) but, *Always taking out of the Meal-Tub, and never putting in soon comes to the Bottom*; then, as *Poor Dick* says, *When the Well's dry they know the Worth of Water.* But this they might have known before, if they had taken his Advice. *If you would know the Value of Money, go and try to borrow some*; for, *He that goes a borrow-*

Father *Abraham*'s Speech.

ing goes a sorrowing ; and indeed so does he that
lends to such People, when he goes *to get it in
again.*----*Poor Dick* farther advises and says,

  Fond Pride of Dress, *is sure a very Curse.*

  E'er Fancy *yon consult, consult your Purse.*

And again, *Pride is as loud a Beggar as Want,
and a great deal more saucy.* When you have bought
one fine Thing you must buy ten more, that your
Appearance may be all of a Piece ; but Poor *Dick*
says, *'Tis easier to* suppress *the first Desire, than to*
satisfy *all that follow it.* And 'tis as truly Folly
for the Poor to *ape* the Rich, as for the Frog to
swell in order to equal the Ox,

  Great Estates may venture more,

  But little Boats should keep near Shore.

'Tis however a Folly soon punished ; for *Pride that
dines on Vanity sups on Contempt,* as Poor *Richard*
says. And, in another Place, *Pride breakfasted
with Plenty, dined with Poverty, and supped with
Infamy.* And, after all, of what Use is this *Pride
of Appearance,* for which so much is risqued, so
much is suffered ? It cannot promote Health, or
ease Pain ; it makes no Increase of Merit in the
Person ; it creates Envy, it hastens Misfortune.

  What is a Butterfly? At best

  He's but a Catterpillar drest.

  The gaudy Fop's his Picture just ;

as Poor *Richard* says.

  But what Madness must it be to *run in Debt* for
these Superfluities ! We are offered, by the Terms

ing goes a sorrowing; and indeed so does he that lends to such people, when he goes *to get it in again.*—*Poor Dick* farther advises, and says,

> *Fond* Pride if Dress, *is sure a very Curse.*
> *E'er* Fancy *you consult, consult your Purse.*

And again, *Pride is as loud a Beggar as Want, and a great deal more saucy.* When you have bought one fine Thing you must buy ten more, that your Appearance maybe all of a Piece; but Poor *Dick* says, *'Tis easier to* suppress *the first desire, than to* satisfy *all that follow it.* And 'tis as truly Folly for the Poor to *ape* the Rich, as for the Frog to swell, in order to equal the Ox.

> *Great Estates may venture more,*
> *But little Boats should keep near Shore.*

'Tis however a Folly soon punished; for *Pride that dines on Vanity sups on Contempt*, as Poor *Richard* says. And in another Place, *Pride breakfasted with Plenty, dined with Poverty, and supped with Infamy.* And, after all, of what Use is this *Pride of Appearance*, for which so much is risked, so much is suffered? It cannot promote Health; or ease Pain; it makes no Increase of Merit in the Person; it creates Envy, it hastens Misfortune.

> *What is a Butterfly? At best*
> *He's but a Caterpillar dressed.*
> *The gaudy Fop's his Picture just,*

as Poor Richard says.

But what Madness must it be to *run in Debt* for these Superfluities! We are offered, by the Terms

Father *Abraham*'s Speech.

of this Vendue, *Six Months Credit*; and that, perhaps, has induced some of us to attend it, because we cannot spare the ready Money, and hope now to be fine without it. But, ah! think what you do when you run in Debt: *You give to another Power over your Liberty.* If you cannot pay at the Time, you will be ashamed to see your Creditor; you will be in Fear when you speak to him; you will make poor, pitiful, sneaking Excuses, and by Degrees come to lose your Veracity, and sink into base downright Lying; for, as Poor *Richard* says, *The second Vice is Lying, the first is running in Debt.* And again, to the same Purpose, *Lying rides upon Debt's Back.* Whereas a freeborn *Englishman* ought not to be ashamed or afraid to see or speak to any Man living. But Poverty often deprives a Man of all Spirit and Virtue. *'Tis hard for an empty Bag to stand upright,* as Poor *Richard* truly says. What would you think of that Prince, or that Government, who should issue an Edict forbiding you to dress like a Gentleman or a Gentlewoman, on Pain of Imprisonment or Servitude? Would you not say that you are free, have a Right to dress as you please, and that such an Edict would be a Breach of your Privileges, and such a Government tyrannical? And yet you are about to put yourself under that Tyranny, when you run in Debt for such Dress! Your Creditor has Authority, at his Pleasure, to deprive you of your Liberty, by confining you in Goal for Life, of this Vendue, *Six Months Credit*; and that, perhaps, has induced some of us to attend it, because we cannot spare the ready Money, and hope now to be fine without it. But, ah! think what you do when you run in Debt: *You give to another Power over your liberty.* If you cannot pay at the Time, you will be ashamed to see your Creditor; you will be in Fear when you speak to him; you will make poor, pitiful, sneaking Excuses, and by Degrees come to lose your Veracity,and sink into base downright Lying; for, as Poor *Richard* says, *The Second Vice is Lying, the first is running in Debt.* And again, to the same Purpose, *Lying rides upon Debt's back.* Whereas a freeborn *Englishman* ought not to be ashamed or afraid to see or speak to any Man living. But Poverty often deprives a Man of all Spirit and Virtue. *'Tis hard for an empty Bag to stand upright*, as *Poor Richard* truly says. What would you think of that Prince, or that Government, who should issue an Edict forbidding you to dress like a Gentleman or Gentlewoman, on Pain of Imprisonment or Servitude? Would you not say that you are free, have a Right to dress as you please, and that such an Edict would be a Breach of your Privileges, and such a Government tyrannical? And yet you are about to put yourself under that Tyranny when you run in Debt for such Dress! Your Creditor has Authority, at his Pleasure, to deprive you of your Liberty, by confining you in Jail for Life,

Father *Abraham*'s Speech.

or to fell you for a Servant, if you fhould not be able to pay him! When you have got your Bargain, you may, perhaps, think little of Payment; but *Creditors* (Poor *Richard* tells us) *have better Memories than Debtors*; and in another Place fays, *Creditors are a fuperftitious Sect, great Obfervers of fet Days and Times.* The Day comes round before you are aware, and the Demand is made before you are prepared to fatisfy it. Or if you bear your Debt in Mind, the Term which at firft feemed fo long, will, as it leffens, appear extremely fhort. *Time* will feem to have added Wings to his Heels as well as Shoulders. *Thofe have a fhort Lent* (faith *Poor Richard*) *who owe Money to be paid at Eafter.* Then fince, as he fays, *The Borrower is a Slave to the Lender, and the Debtor to the Creditor*, difdain the Chain, preferve your Freedom, and maintain your Independency. Be *induftrious* and *free*; be *frugal* and *free*. At prefent perhaps you may think yourfelf in thriving Circumftances, and that you can bear a little Extravagance without Injury; but

For Age and Want fave while you may.

No Morning-Sun lafts a whole Day;
as *Poor Richard* fays.----Gain may be temporary and uncertain, but ever while you live, Expence is conftant and certain; and *'Tis eafier to build two Chimnies, than to keep one in Fuel*, as *Poor Richard* fays. So *rather go to Bed fupperlefs than rife in Debt.*

Get what you can, and what you get hold;
'Tis the Stone that will turn all your Lead into Gold.
as Poor *Richard* fays.

or to sell you for a Servant, if you should not be able to pay him! When you have got your Bargain, you may, perhaps, think little of Payment; but *Creditors* (Poor *Richard* tells us) *have better Memories than Debtors*; and in another Place says, *Creditors are a superstitious Sect, great Observers of set Days and Times*. The Day comes round before you are aware, and the Demand is made before you are prepared to satisfy it. Or if you bear your Debt in Mind, the Term which at first seemed so long, will, as it lessens, appear extremely short. *Time* will seem to have added Wings to his Heels as well as Shoulders. *Those have a short Lent* (saith *Poor Richard*) *who owe Money to be paid at Easter*. Then since, as he says, *The Borrower is a Slave to the Lender, and the Debtor to the Creditor*, disdain the Chain, preserve your Freedom; and maintain your Independency. Be *industrious* and *free*; be *frugal* and *free*. At present perhaps you may think yourself in thriving Circumstances, and that you can bear a little Extravagance without Injury; but,

> *For Age and Want, save while you may;*
> *No Morning-Sun lasts a whole Day;*

as *Poor Richard* says.—Gain may be temporary and uncertain, but ever while you live, Expense is constant and certain; and *'Tis easier to build two Chimneys, than to keep one in Fuel*, as *Poor Richard* says. So *rather go to Bed supperless than rise in Debt.*

> *Get what you can, and what you get hold;*
> *'Tis the Stone that will turn all your Lead into Gold*, as Poor *Richard* says.

Father *Abraham's* Speech.

And when you have got the Philosopher's Stone, sure you will no longer complain of bad Times, or the Difficulty of paying Taxes.

This Doctrine, my Friends, is *Reason* and *Wisdom*; but, after all, do not depend too much upon your own *Industry*, and *Frugality*, and *Prudence*, though excellent Things, for they may all be blasted without the Blessing of Heaven; and therefore ask that Blessing humbly, and be not uncharitable to those that at present seem to want it, but comfort and help them. Remember *Job* suffered, and was afterwards prosperous.

And now to conclude. *Experience keeps a dear School, but Fools will learn in no other, and scarce in that*; for it is true, *We may give Advice, but we cannot give Conduct*, as *Poor Richard* says: However, remember this, *They that won't be counselled, can't be helped*, as *Poor Richard* says: And farther, that *If you will not hear Reason she'll surely rap your Knuckles.*"

Thus the old Gentleman ended his Harangue. The People heard it, and approved the Doctrine, and immediately practised the Contrary, just as if it had been a common Sermon; for the Vendue opened, and they began to buy extravagantly, notwithstanding all his Cautions, and their own Fear of Taxes.----I found the good Man had thoroughly studied my Almanacks, and digested all I had dropt on those Topicks during the Course of five-and-

And when you have got the Philosopher's Stone, sure you will no longer complain of bad Times, or the Difficulty of paying Taxes.

This Doctrine, my Friends, is *Reason* and *Wisdom*; but, after all, do not depend too much upon your own *Industry*, and *Frugality*, and *Prudence*, though excellent Things, for they may all be blasted without the Blessing of Heaven; and therefore ask that Blessing humbly, and be not uncharitable to those that at present seem to want it, but comfort and help them. Remember *Job* suffered, and was afterwards prosperous.

And now to conclude. *Experience keeps a dear School, but Fools will learn in no other, and scarce in that;* for it is true, *We may give Advice, but we cannot give Conduct,* as *Poor Richard* says: However, remember this, *They that won't be counseled, can't be helped,* as *Poor Richard* says: And farther, that *If you will not hear Reason, she'll surely rap your Knuckles."*

Thus the old Gentleman ended his Harangue. The People heard it, and approved the Doctrine, and immediately practiced the Contrary, just as if it had been a common Sermon; for the Vendue opened, and they began to buy extravagantly, notwithstanding all his Cautions, and their own Fear of Taxes.—I found the good Man had thoroughly studied my Almanacks, and digested all I had dropped on those Topics during the Course of five-and-

Poor *Richard*'s Conclusion.

twenty Years. The frequent Mention he made of me, muſt have tired any one elſe, but my Vanity was wonderfully delighted with it, though I was conſcious that not a tenth Part of the Wiſdom was my own which he aſcribed to me, but rather the *Gleanings* I had made of the Senſe of all Ages and Nations. However, I reſolved to be the better for the Echo of it ; and thô I had at firſt determined to buy Stuff for a new Coat, I went away reſolved to wear my old One a little longer. *Reader*, if thou wilt do the ſame, thy Profit will be as great as mine.

I am, as ever,

Thine to ſerve thee,

Richard Saunders.

July 7. 1757

twenty Years. The frequent Mention he made of me, must have tired any one else, but my Vanity was wonderfully delighted with it, though I was conscious that not a tenth Part of the Wisdom was my own which he ascribed to me, but rather the *Gleanings* I had made of the Sense of all Ages and Nations. However, I resolved to be the better for the Echo of it; and though I had at first determined to buy Stuff for a new Coat, I went away resolved to wear my old One a little longer. *Reader*, if thou wilt do the same, thy Profit will be as great as mine.

I am, as ever,

Thine to serve thee,

Richard Saunders

July 7, 1757

MAIN EVENTS IN FRANKLIN'S LIFE

1706 He is born, in Boston, and baptized in the Old South Church.

1714 At the age of eight, enters the Grammar School.

1716 Becomes his father's assistant in the tallow-chandlery business.

1718 Apprenticed to his brother James, printer.

1721 Writes ballads and peddles them, in printed form, in the streets; contributes, anonymously, to the *New England Courant*, and temporarily edits that paper; becomes a free-thinker, and a vegetarian.

1723 Breaks his indenture and removes to Philadelphia; obtaining employment in Keimer's printing office; abandons vegetarianism.

1724 Is persuaded by Governor Keith to establish himself independently, and goes to London to buy type; works at

135

his trade there, and publishes "Dissertation on Liberty and Necessity, Pleasure and Pain."

1726 Returns to Philadelphia; after serving as clerk in a dry goods store, becomes manager of Keimer's printing house.

1727 Founds the Junto, or "Leathern Apron" Club.

1728 With Hugh Meredith, opens a printing office.

1729 Becomes proprietor and editor of the *Pennsylvania Gazette*; prints, anonymously, "Nature and Necessity of a Paper Currency;" opens a stationer's shop.

1730 Marries Rebecca Read.

1731 Founds the Philadelphia Library.

1732 Publishes the first number of *Poor Richard's Almanack* under the pseudonym of "Richard Saunders." The *Almanack*, which continued for twenty-five years to contain his witty, worldly-wise sayings, played a very large part in bringing together and molding the American character which was at that time made up of so many diverse and scattered types.

1733 Begins to study French, Italian, Spanish, and Latin.

1736 Chosen clerk of the General Assembly; forms the Union Fire Company of Philadelphia.

1737 Elected to the Assembly; appointed Deputy Postmaster General; plans a city police.

1742 Invents the open, or "Franklin," stove.

1743 Proposes a plan for an Academy, which is adopted in 1749 and develops into the University of Pennsylvania.

1744 Establishes the American Philosophical Society.

1746 Publishes a pamphlet, "Plain Truth," on the necessity for disciplined defense, and forms a military company; begins electrical experiments.

1748 Sells out his printing business; is appointed on the Commission of the Peace, chosen to the Common Council, and to the Assembly.

1749 Appointed a Commissioner to trade with the Indians.

1751 Aids in founding a hospital.

1752 Experiments with a kite and discovers that lightning is an electrical discharge.

1753 Awarded the Copley medal for this discovery, and elected a member of the Royal Society; receives the degree of MA from Yale and Harvard. Appointed joint Postmaster General.

1754 Appointed one of the Commissioners from Pennsylvania to the Colonial Congress at Albany; proposes a plan for the union of the colonies.

1755 Pledges his personal property in order that supplies may be raised for Braddock's army; obtains a grant from the Assembly in aid of the Crown Point expedition; carries through a bill establishing a voluntary militia; is appointed Colonel, and takes the field.

1757 Introduces a bill in the Assembly for paving the streets of Philadelphia; publishes his famous "Way to Wealth"; goes to England to plead the cause of the Assembly against the Proprietaries; remains as agent for Pennsylvania; enjoys the friendship of the scientific and literary men of the kingdom.

1760 Secures from the Privy Council, by a compromise, a decision obliging the Proprietary estates to contribute to the public revenue.

1762 Receives the degree of LL.D. from Oxford and Edinburgh; returns to America.

1763 Makes a five months' tour of the northern colonies for the Purpose of inspecting the post offices.

1764 Defeated by the Penn faction for reelection to the Assembly; sent to England as agent for Pennsylvania.

1765 Endeavors to prevent the passage of the Stamp Act.

1766 Examined before the House of Commons relative to the passage of the Stamp Act; appointed agent of Massachusetts, New Jersey, and Georgia; visits Gottingen University.

1767 Travels in France and is presented at court.

1769 Procures a telescope for Harvard College.

1772 Elected *Associé Étranger* of the French Academy.

1774 Dismissed from the office of Postmaster General; influences Thomas Paine to emigrate to America.

1775 Returns to America; chosen a delegate to the Second Continental Congress; placed on the committee of secret correspondence; appointed one of the commissioners to secure the cooperation of Canada.

1776 Placed on the committee to draft a Declaration of Independence; chosen president of the Constitutional Committee of Pennsylvania; sent to France as agent of the colonies.

1778 Concludes treaties of defensive alliance, and of amity and commerce; is received at court.

1779 Appointed Minister Plenipotentiary to France.

1780 Appoints Paul Jones commander of the "Alliance."

1782 Signs the preliminary articles of peace.

1783 Signs the definite treaty of peace.

1785 Returns to America; is chosen President of Pennsylvania; reelected 1786.

1787 Reelected President; sent as delegate to the convention for framing a Federal Constitution.

1788 Retires from public life.

1790 April 17, dies. His grave is in the churchyard at Fifth and Arch streets, Philadelphia.

SOURCES

"Chief Events in Franklin's Life." *Sparknotes Classic Books: The Autobiography of Benjamin Franklin.* New York: SparkNotes LLC, 2003.
<http://pd.sparknotes.com/lit/franklinautobio/>.

Hornung, Clarence P. *Handbook of Early Advertising Art: Mainly From American Art, Third Edition.* New York: Dover Publications Inc., 1956.

Humes, James C. *The Wit & Wisdom of Benjamin Franklin: A Treasury of More Than 900 Quotations and Anecdotes.* New York: HarperCollins Publishers, 1995.

Isaacson, Walter, Editor. *A Benjamin Franklin Reader.* New York: Simon & Schuster, 2003.

Isaacson, Walter. *Benjamin Franklin: An American Life.* New York: Simon & Schuster, 2003.

Labaree, Leonard W. and Whitfield J. Bell, Jr., Editors. *Mr Franklin: A Selection from His Personal Letters.* New Haven, Connecticut: Yale University Press, 1956.

Van Doren, Carl, Editor. *Benjamin Franklin's Autobiographical Writings.* New York: The History Book Club, Viking Press, 1948.